ZICKZACK

CW01652339

Was kannst du? 1B

Testmaterial

Bryan Goodman-Stephens,
Paul Rogers, Lol Briggs.

Teacher's Book

Nelson

Thomas Nelson and Sons Ltd
Nelson House Mayfield Road
Walton-on-Thames Surrey
KT12 5PL UK

51 York Place
Edinburgh
EH1 3JD UK

Thomas Nelson (Hong Kong) Ltd
Toppan Building 10/F
22A Westlands Road
Quarry Bay Hong Kong

Thomas Nelson Australia
102 Dodds Street
South Melbourne Victoria 3205
Australia

Nelson Canada
1120 Birchmount Road
Scarborough Ontario
M1K 5G4 Canada

©Bryan Goodman-Stephens, Paul Rogers, Lol Briggs 1990

First published by Thomas Nelson and Sons Ltd 1990

ISBN 0-17-439250-8

NPN 9 8 7 6 5 4 3 2

All rights reserved. No paragraph of this publication may be reproduced, copied or transmitted save with written permission or in accordance with the provisions of the Copyright, Design and Patents Act 1988, or under the terms of any licence permitting limited copying issued by the Copyright Licensing Agency, 33-34 Alfred Place, London WC1E 7DP.

Any person who does any unauthorised act in relation to this publication may be liable to criminal prosecution and civil claims for damages.

Printed and bound in Great Britain by
Hobbs the Printers of Southampton

Contents

Introduction

The ***Zickzack*** assessment materials, entitled ***Was kannst du? 1B***, cover chapters 7 to 12 of Stage 1. They have been designed to enable teachers and pupils to evaluate pupil progress quickly and efficiently. Extensive use has been made of visuals to support understanding and increase motivation.

1 Contents of the package

There is a test, covering all four skill areas, for each chapter, with a maximum score of 50 marks. The greatest emphasis is placed upon the skills of Listening, Reading and Speaking. Additionally there are two cumulative tests, covering all four skills in chapters 7-9 and 7-12 respectively, with a maximum score of 100 marks each. Whilst the emphasis, as in the chapter tests, is still on positive achievement, the cumulative tests are more discriminating. Results of all tests are collated on a profile sheet which consists of a series of positive statements of achievement.

2 Conduct of the tests

The test items have clear rubrics and, in most instances, start with an example in order to ensure that pupils know precisely what to do. It should be possible to conduct the Listening, Reading and Writing tests in the space of a single lesson each. The Speaking tests lend themselves readily to pairwork assessment and can, therefore, also be conducted quickly and efficiently. Of course, if teachers prefer, the speaking tests can be conducted by the teacher, face-to-face with individual pupils.

3 Marking

Solutions and mark schemes are included throughout for all tests. Generally, in order to avoid ambiguity, open-ended questions have not been used. Answers can be checked quickly, since they are often in the form of ticked boxes, true-false format or single word responses. The Speaking tests provide pupils with ample opportunity to score full marks, as the total number of points available to them exceeds the maximum. The teacher can adopt the marking scheme suggested with each speaking test or alternatively a 2 - 1 - 0 system could be adopted:

2 marks - meaning accurately conveyed
1 mark - meaning clear to sympathetic native speaker, but some mistakes
0 marks - meaning not communicated

e.g. Asking your partner about him/herself
Wie heißt du? 2 marks
Wie heiße du? 1 mark
Dein Name? 1 mark
Du Name? 0 marks
Heiße? 0 marks
The marks may then need to be scaled to the final total for that test.

4 Profiles

The profile sheets enable pupils to keep a record of their progress from chapter to chapter. The brief statements about what pupils can do are accompanied by a notional mastery score (i.e. the level of understanding, knowledge or skill required to complete the task successfully). These sheets also help pupils to develop a critical awareness of their learning and performance by inviting comments on the appeal of the chapter concerned and the areas in which they feel they could improve.

5 Certification

On completion of the appropriate tests pupils may be awarded a Zickzack certificate of achievement, which indicates clearly the areas in which pupils have demonstrated competence.

Kapitel 7

HÖREN

A Understanding directions (1)

Tests comprehension of simple directions.

Wo ist die Post?

Beispiel:
– Entschuldigung. Wo ist die Post?
– Hier links.
– Ach ja. Danke.

1 – Entschuldigung. Ist hier ein Kino in der Nähe?
– Ein Kino? Ja, hier um die Ecke.
– Ja. Danke.
2 – Entschuldigung. Ich suche einen Parkplatz.
– Na ja, der nächste Parkplatz ist hier geradeaus.
3 – Entschuldigung. Wo ist hier das Krankenhaus?
– Das Krankenhaus? Das ist ganz einfach. Sie gehen hier rechts.
– Danke schön.
– Gern geschehen.
4 – Gibt es ein Jugendzentrum hier in der Nähe?
– Na klar. Da drüben.
– Toll. Vielen Dank.
– Bitte.
5 – Entschuldigung, wo ist hier die nächste Bank?
– Das ist hier gleich um die Ecke.
– Danke schön.
6 – Entschuldigung.
– Ja?
– Wo ist die nächste Bushaltestelle?
– Sie gehen hier links.
– Oh, danke.
– Nichts zu danken.

Solution:
1 round the corner
2 straight ahead
3 right
4 over there
5 round the corner
6 left
Total: **6**

B Understanding directions (2)

Wo ist der Bahnhof?

Beispiel:
– Entschuldigung. Wo ist der Bahnhof?
– Hier bis zur Ampel und dann rechts.
– Vielen Dank.

1 – Entschuldigung. Wo ist hier die Fußgängerzone?
– Die Fußgängerzone? Ja, das ist ganz einfach. Hier geradeaus, dann die zweite Straße links rein, auf der rechten Seite.
– Also – geradeaus, dann die zweite Straße links. Danke schön.
– Bitte sehr.
2 – Entschuldigung ... wo ist hier der Dom? Wie komme ich am besten dahin?
– Nehmen Sie die dritte Straße rechts. Der Dom ist auf der linken Seite.
– Ist das weit von hier?
– Ja, ziemlich weit. Zehn Minuten zu Fuß.
– Ach, das geht schon. Danke.
3 – Wir suchen eine Disko. Gibt's hier eine in der Nähe?
– Eine Disko? Ja, ihr geht hier links, dann geradeaus. Dann biegt ihr rechts ab – das heißt, die erste Straße rechts. Dann seht ihr eine Disko auf der linken Seite.
– Also hier links, dann die erste Straße rechts. Danke. Tschüs.
– Tschüs.
4 – Entschuldigung.
– Ja.
– Wo ist die Stadthalle?
– Sind Sie zu Fuß, oder ... ?
– Ja.
– Es ist nämlich ziemlich weit. Sie gehen hier geradeaus, ungefähr zwei Kilometer, dann biegen Sie am Bahnhof rechts ab. Die Stadthalle sehen Sie dann auf der linken Seite.
– Also geradeaus, dann am Bahnhof rechts ab. Danke sehr.
– Bitte sehr.

Solution:
See reduction
Total: **4**

C Understanding directions (3)

Tests comprehension of distances/times.

Ist es weit von hier?

Beispiel:
– Ich suche das Verkehrsamt. Ist es weit von hier?
– Nein, nicht weit. Hundert Meter oder so. Sie gehen hier geradeaus.
– Danke.
– Bitte.

1 – Ich suche den Sportplatz. Ist es weit von hier?
– Ja, ziemlich weit. Am besten fahren Sie mit der Straßenbahn, also mit der Nummer elf. Sie fahren vier Stationen – das heißt ungefähr fünfzehn Minuten.
– Danke.
2 – Entschuldigung. Wo ist die Tennishalle?
– Die Tennishalle suchen Sie? Das ist nicht weit, vielleicht vierhundert Meter. Hier diese Straße entlang und dann links.
– Danke.
– Bitte.
3 – Entschuldigung. Ist die Jugendherberge weit von hier?
– Die Jugendherberge? Das ist sehr weit. Vielleicht fünf Kilometer ... aber ein Bus fährt dahin.

Solution:
1H **2**G **3**B
Total: **3**

D Understanding conversations at the Tourist Information Office

Im Verkehrsamt

Beispiel:
– Guten Morgen.
– Guten Morgen. Haben Sie hier Informationen über Kinos?
– Ja natürlich.
– Und auch über Theaterkarten?
– Ja, die kann man hier kaufen.

1 – Guten Tag.
– Guten Tag.
– Ich möchte einen Stadtplan und ein Hotelverzeichnis.
– Ja ... bitte schön.
– Danke. Haben Sie auch Informationsmaterial über Ausflüge?
– Ja, natürlich. Bitte schön.
– Danke. Was kostet das?
– Das ist alles kostenlos.
– Oh, vielen Dank.
– Bitte schön. Auf Wiedersehen.
– Auf Wiedersehen.
2 – Guten Morgen. Ich möchte einen Prospekt über die Stadt.
– So, bitte schön.
– Danke. Haben Sie auch Informationen über Restaurants?
– Ja, hier haben Sie ein Verzeichnis.
– Danke schön.
3 – Guten Tag. Ich bin erst seit gestern abend hier in der Stadt. Könnte ich bitte eine Broschüre haben und das Poster da?
– Bitte schön.
– Was kostet das?
– Die Broschüre ist gratis, und das Poster kostet DM 2,50.
– So ... ach ja, was kostet das Buch da?
– Das Buch über die Stadt?
– Ja.
– DM 15,90.
– Ja, das nehme ich auch.

Solution:
1 a G **b** D **c** B **2 a** A **b** F **3 a** H **b** E **c** J
Total: **8**

LESEN

E Understanding what people write about themselves and their town

Tests comprehension of short texts about people in the town of Cologne.

Solution:
Christian T.; Österreich; Student; (in der) Innenstadt
Helga M.; Bonn; Taxifahrerin; (am) Stadtrand
Kurt H.; Leipzig; —; (in einem) Altersheim (am Stadtrand)
Total: **9**

F Understanding signs

Tests comprehension of traffic signs.

Solution:

youth hostel **E**	hospital —
police station —	castle **A**
railway station **B**	town hall **C**
tourist office **F**	Total: **5**

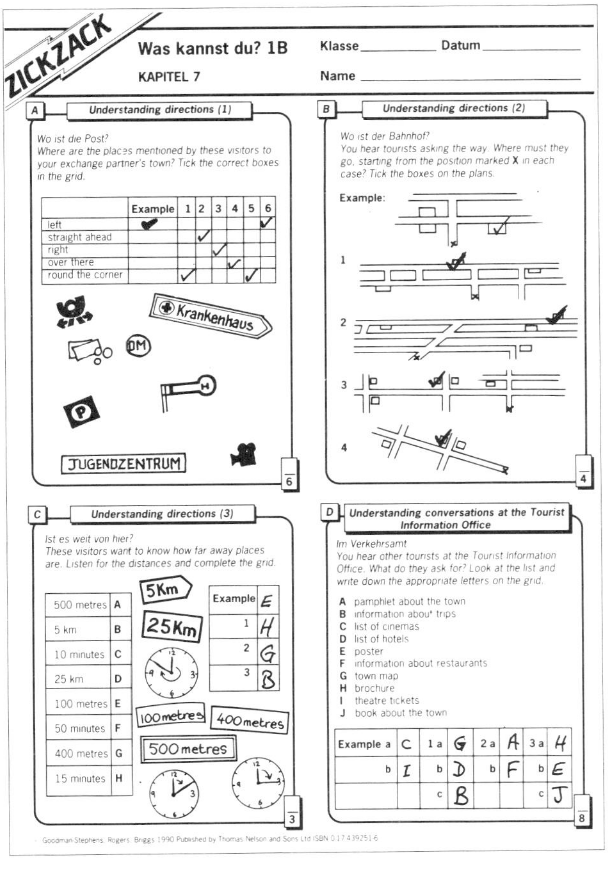
ZICKZACK

Was kannst du? 1B Klasse ______ Datum ______

KAPITEL 7 Name ______

A Understanding directions (1)

Wo ist die Post?
Where are the places mentioned by these visitors to your exchange partner's town? Tick the correct boxes in the grid.

	Example	1	2	3	4	5	6
left	✓						✓
straight ahead			✓				
right				✓			
over there					✓		
round the corner		✓				✓	

6

B Understanding directions (2)

Wo ist der Bahnhof?
*You hear tourists asking the way. Where must they go, starting from the position marked **X** in each case? Tick the boxes on the plans.*

Example:
1
2
3
4
4

C Understanding directions (3)

Ist es weit von hier?
These visitors want to know how far away places are. Listen for the distances and complete the grid.

500 metres	A
5 km	B
10 minutes	C
25 km	D
100 metres	E
50 minutes	F
400 metres	G
15 minutes	H

Example	E
1	H
2	G
3	B

3

D Understanding conversations at the Tourist Information Office

Im Verkehrsamt
You hear other tourists at the Tourist Information Office. What do they ask for? Look at the list and write down the appropriate letters on the grid.

A pamphlet about the town
B information about trips
C list of cinemas
D list of hotels
E poster
F information about restaurants
G town map
H brochure
I theatre tickets
J book about the town

Example a	C	1 a	G	2 a	A	3 a	H
b	I	b	D	b	F	b	E
		c	B			c	J

8

Goodman-Stephens, Rogers, Briggs 1990 Published by Thomas Nelson and Sons Ltd ISBN 0-17-439251-6

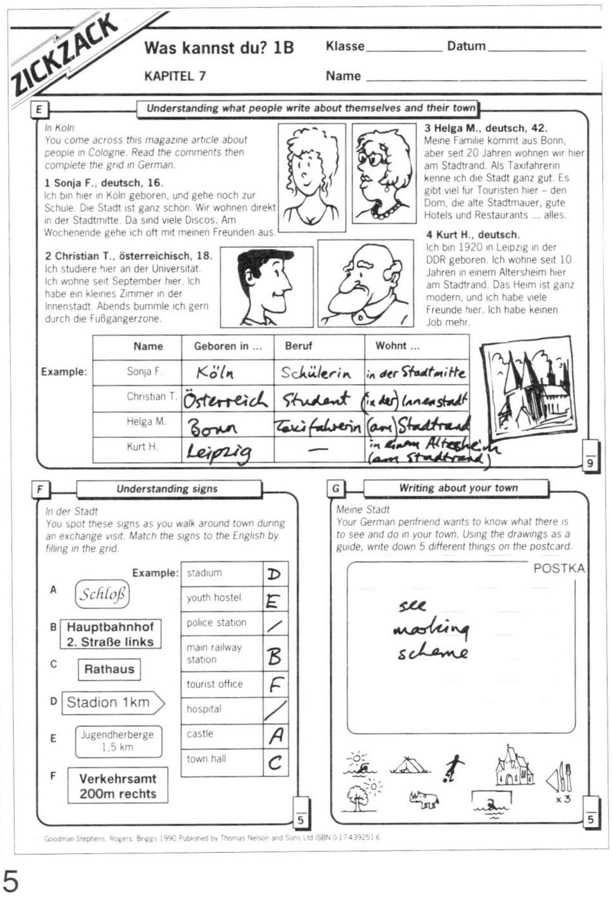
ZICKZACK

Was kannst du? 1B Klasse ______ Datum ______

KAPITEL 7 Name ______

E Understanding what people write about themselves and their town

In Köln
You come across this magazine article about people in Cologne. Read the comments then complete the grid in German.

1 Sonja F., deutsch, 16.
Ich bin hier in Köln geboren, und gehe noch zur Schule. Die Stadt ist ganz schön. Wir wohnen direkt in der Stadtmitte. Da sind viele Discos. Am Wochenende gehe ich oft mit meinen Freunden aus.

2 Christian T., österreichisch, 18.
Ich studiere hier an der Universität. Ich wohne seit September hier. Ich habe ein kleines Zimmer in der Innenstadt. Abends bummle ich gern durch die Fußgängerzone.

3 Helga M., deutsch, 42.
Meine Familie kommt aus Bonn, aber seit 20 Jahren wohnen wir hier am Stadtrand. Als Taxifahrerin kenne ich die Stadt ganz gut. Es gibt viel für Touristen hier – den Dom, die alte Stadtmauer, gute Hotels und Restaurants ... alles.

4 Kurt H., deutsch.
Ich bin 1920 in Leipzig in der DDR geboren. Ich wohne seit 10 Jahren in einem Altersheim hier am Stadtrand. Das Heim ist ganz modern, und ich habe viele Freunde hier. Ich habe keinen Job mehr.

	Name	Geboren in ...	Beruf	Wohnt ...
Example:	Sonja F.	Köln	Schülerin	in der Stadtmitte
	Christian T.	Österreich	Student	(in der) Innenstadt
	Helga M.	Bonn	Taxifahrerin	(am) Stadtrand
	Kurt H.	Leipzig	—	in einem Altersheim (am Stadtrand)

9

F Understanding signs

In der Stadt
You spot these signs as you walk around town during an exchange visit. Match the signs to the English by filling in the grid.

A Schloß
B Hauptbahnhof 2. Straße links
C Rathaus
D Stadion 1km
E Jugendherberge 1,5 km
F Verkehrsamt 200m rechts

Example:	stadium	D
	youth hostel	E
	police station	/
	main railway station	B
	tourist office	F
	hospital	/
	castle	A
	town hall	C

5

G Writing about your town

Meine Stadt
Your German penfriend wants to know what there is to see and do in your town. Using the drawings as a guide, write down 5 different things on the postcard.

POSTKA

see marking scheme

x 3

5

Goodman-Stephens, Rogers, Briggs 1990 Published by Thomas Nelson and Sons Ltd ISBN 0-17-439251-6

SCHREIBEN

G Writing about your town

Tests ability to write down town facilities/ buildings on a postcard to a penfriend.

Marking scheme:
Any 5 buildings/establishments. 1 mark each for communication.
Total: **5**

SPRECHEN

H Asking for and giving directions

Tests the ability to ask questions and give information about directions.
Three different sets of pairwork materials. Two activities per pupil in pairwork.
Pupils should be given one of the roles and should then work either with a partner or with the teacher (see Introduction).

Marking scheme:
1 mark per item up to a maximum of 10

1A Gehen Sie / hier geradeaus/ **2**
nehmen Sie / die erste Straße / rechts **3**
Nein, fünfhundert Meter **2**
Entschuldigung, / wo ist hier / das Schwimmbad / Freibad / Hallenbad? **3**
Ist es weit / von hier? **2**
Total: **10** (maximum)

1B Entschuldigung, / wo ist hier / die Jugendherberge? **3**
Ist es weit / von hier? **2**
Gehen Sie / hier geradeaus, / nehmen Sie / **3**
die erste Straße / rechts und (dann) / **2**
die dritte (Straße) rechts **1**
Ja, ein Kilometer **1**
Total: **10** (maximum)

2A Nehmen Sie / die erste Straße / links / und die zweite Straße / rechts **5**
Nein, sechshundert Meter **1**
Entschuldigung, / wo ist hier / die Post? **3**
Ist es weit / von hier? **2**
Total: **10** (maximum)

2B Entschuldigung, / wo ist hier / das Verkehrsamt? **3**
Ist es weit / von hier? **2**
Nehmen Sie / die erste Straße / rechts / und die erste Straße / links und (dann) / wieder die erste Straße rechts **6**
Nein, achthundert Meter **1**
Total: **10** (maximum)

3A Nehmen Sie / die erste Straße / links / und die zweite Straße / rechts **5**
Ja, zwei Kilometer **1**
Entschuldigung, / wo ist hier / der Campingplatz? **3**
Ist es weit / von hier? **2**
Total: **10** (maximum)

3B Entschuldigung, / wo ist hier / der Bahnhof? **3**
Ist es weit / von hier? **2**
Gehen Sie / hier geradeaus / nehmen Sie / die zweite Straße / rechts / die erste Straße / **3**
links / und (dann wieder) die erste Straße links **2**
Ja, drei Kilometer **1**
Total: **10** (maximum)

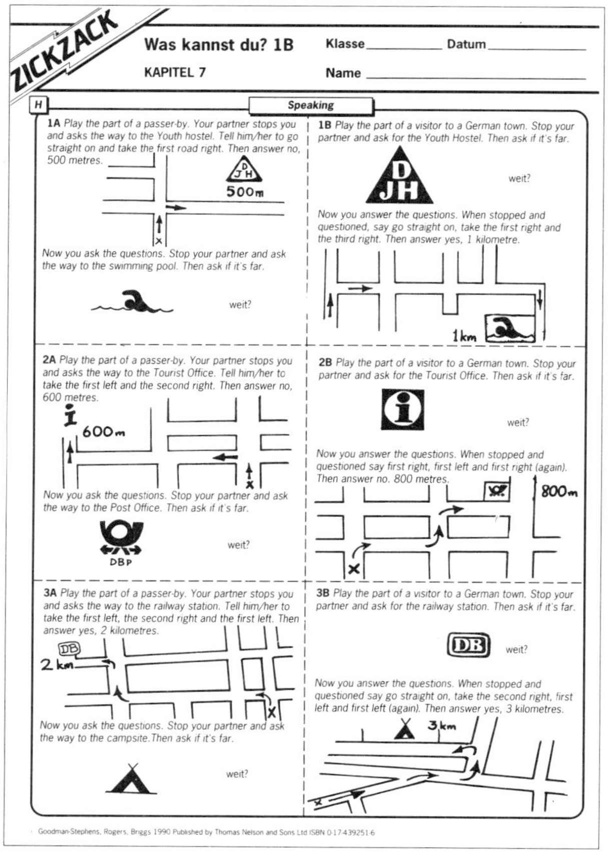
ZICKZACK
Was kannst du? 1B — Klasse ______ Datum ______
KAPITEL 7 — Name ______

H — Speaking

1A Play the part of a passer-by. Your partner stops you and asks the way to the Youth hostel. Tell him/her to go straight on and take the first road right. Then answer no, 500 metres.

Now you ask the questions. Stop your partner and ask the way to the swimming pool. Then ask if it's far.
weit?

1B Play the part of a visitor to a German town. Stop your partner and ask for the Youth Hostel. Then ask if it's far.

weit?
Now you answer the questions. When stopped and questioned, say go straight on, take the first right and the third right. Then answer yes, 1 kilometre.

2A Play the part of a passer-by. Your partner stops you and asks the way to the Tourist Office. Tell him/her to take the first left and the second right. Then answer no, 600 metres.

Now you ask the questions. Stop your partner and ask the way to the Post Office. Then ask if it's far.

weit?

2B Play the part of a visitor to a German town. Stop your partner and ask for the Tourist Office. Then ask if it's far.
weit?
Now you answer the questions. When stopped and questioned say first right, first left and first right (again). Then answer no. 800 metres.

3A Play the part of a passer-by. Your partner stops you and asks the way to the railway station. Tell him/her to take the first left, the second right and the first left. Then answer yes, 2 kilometres.

Now you ask the questions. Stop your partner and ask the way to the campsite. Then ask if it's far.
weit?

3B Play the part of a visitor to a German town. Stop your partner and ask for the railway station. Then ask if it's far.

weit?
Now you answer the questions. When stopped and questioned say go straight on, take the second right, first left and first left (again). Then answer yes, 3 kilometres.

Goodman-Stephens, Rogers, Briggs 1990 Published by Thomas Nelson and Sons Ltd ISBN 0-17-439251-6

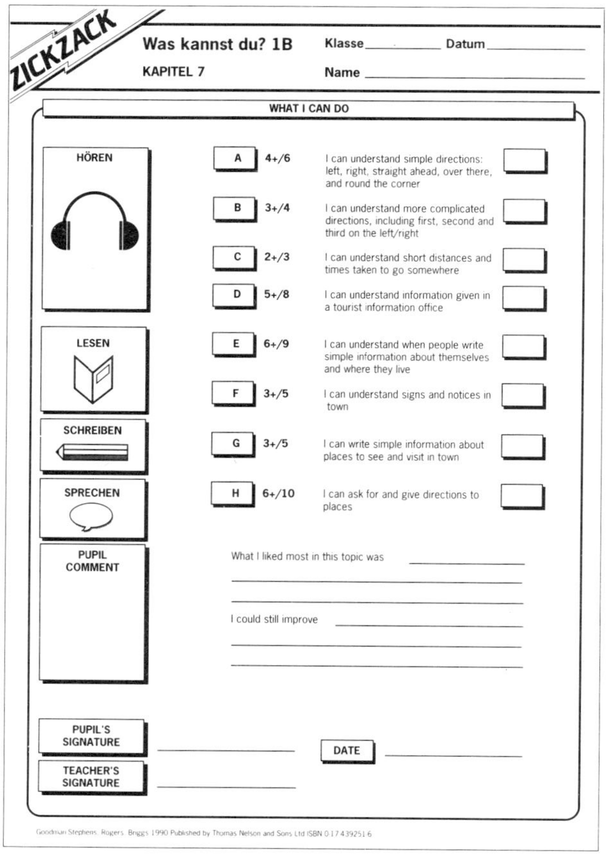
ZICKZACK
Was kannst du? 1B — Klasse ______ Datum ______
KAPITEL 7 — Name ______

WHAT I CAN DO

HÖREN	A	4+/6	I can understand simple directions: left, right, straight ahead, over there, and round the corner	
	B	3+/4	I can understand more complicated directions, including first, second and third on the left/right	
	C	2+/3	I can understand short distances and times taken to go somewhere	
	D	5+/8	I can understand information given in a tourist information office	
LESEN	E	6+/9	I can understand when people write simple information about themselves and where they live	
	F	3+/5	I can understand signs and notices in town	
SCHREIBEN	G	3+/5	I can write simple information about places to see and visit in town	
SPRECHEN	H	6+/10	I can ask for and give directions to places	

PUPIL COMMENT
What I liked most in this topic was ______
I could still improve ______

PUPIL'S SIGNATURE ______ DATE ______
TEACHER'S SIGNATURE ______

Goodman-Stephens, Rogers, Briggs 1990 Published by Thomas Nelson and Sons Ltd ISBN 0-17-439251-6

Kapitel 8

HÖREN

A Understanding talk about buying food and drink

Tests comprehension of food and drink and weights, measures and containers.

Einkaufen

Beispiel:
– Bitte schön?
– Dreihundert Gramm Käse bitte.
– Sonst noch etwas?
– Nein danke.

1 – Was darf's sein?
– Ich möchte eine Packung Kekse.
– So, bitte schön.
2 – Sie wünschen?
– Zehn Kilo Kartoffeln.
– Sonst noch etwas?
– Danke. Das ist alles.
3 – Bitte schön?
– Eine Schachtel Pralinen.
– Sonst noch etwas?
– Ja. Zwei Marsriegel.
4 – Was darf's sein?
– Einen Liter Milch und 500 Gramm Wurst.
– Sonst noch etwas?
– Nein danke.
5 – Guten Tag. Sie wünschen?
– Ein Pfund Karotten.
– So, bitte schön, ein Pfund Karotten. Sonst noch etwas?
– Ja ... ein Kilo Tomaten.
– Bitte schön.
6 – Guten Morgen.
– Guten Morgen. Was darf's sein?
– Ein Glas Honig und einen Becher Margarine.

Solution:
1 true **2** true **3** false **4** false **5** true **6** true
Total: **6**

B Understanding language at the Post Office

Tests comprehension of stamp prices.

Auf der Post

Beispiel:
– Guten Tag. Zehn Briefmarken zu achtzig Pfennig.
– Zehn zu achtzig ... DM 8,- bitte.
1 – Guten Morgen. Fünf Briefmarken zu fünfzig, bitte.
– Bitte schön. Das macht DM 2,50.
2 – Drei Briefmarken zu einer Mark.
– Bitte schön. DM 3,-.
– Bitte.
– Danke.
3 – Vier Briefmarken zu sechzig.
– Vier zu sechzig ... das macht DM 2,40.
– Moment ich hab' das klein.
– Danke.
4 – Eine Briefmarke zu DM 1,20.
– Bitte schön.
– Danke.

Solution:
1B **2**G **3**D **4**A
Total: **4**

C Understanding people saying what they have bought

Tests comprehension of shopping vocabulary.

Was hast du gekauft?

Beispiel:
– Hallo Bernd. Wie geht's?
– Gut danke. Und dir?
– Danke, auch gut. Hast du was Interessantes gekauft?
– Ja, dieses Computerspiel.
– War es teuer?
– Nein, nur DM 25,-.
1 – Grüß dich Gaby. Gehst du in die Stadt?
– Hallo Heidi. Ja. Kommst du mit?
– Nein danke, ich war schon den ganzen Vormittag in der Stadt.
– Ach so. Hast du was gekauft?
– Nur etwas Make-up.
– Sieht gut aus. War es teuer?
– Nein, ganz billig. Es hat nur DM 6,50 gekostet.
2 – Hallo Peter ... na, was hast du gekauft?
– Ein Portemonnaie für meinen Vater. Am Samstag hat er nämlich Geburtstag. Es war wirklich teuer ...
– Was hat's gekostet?
– Fünfzig Mark.
– Fünfzig Mark!!
– Ja, aber es ist aus Leder.
3 – Grüß dich Annette. Wie geht's?
– Ach, ich bin so müde.
– Wieso denn?
– Ich war den ganzen Tag in der Stadt.
– Hast du was Interessantes gekauft?
– Diesen Schal hier.
– Ist er aus Wolle?
– Nein, Polyester. Hat nur DM 9,50 gekostet.

Solution:
1 Heidi: make-up, DM 6,50
2 Peter: wallet, DM 50,-
3 Annette: scarf, DM 9,50
Total: **6**

LESEN

D Understanding names of shops

Tests comprehension of shop names.

Solution:
1E **2**G **3**B **4**F
Total: **4**

E Understanding supermarket goods and price lists

Tests comprehension of supermarket goods and prices.

Solution:

1	7,90	**3**	9,98	**5**	1,79
2	9,99	**4**	0,79	**6**	8,88

Total: **6**

F Understanding a store guide

Tests comprehension of a store guide.

Solution:

	Floor		Floor		Floor		Floor
1	2	**3**	5	**5**	4	**7**	2
2	E	**4**	U	**6**	3	**8**	U

Total: **8**

SCHREIBEN

G Writing

Tests knowledge of items of shopping.

Solution:
... habe ich ein T-Shirt/einen Pullover/Jeans/ Cassetten/Sportschuhe (Trainingsschuhe) gekauft
1 mark each for communication, even with error.
Total: **6**

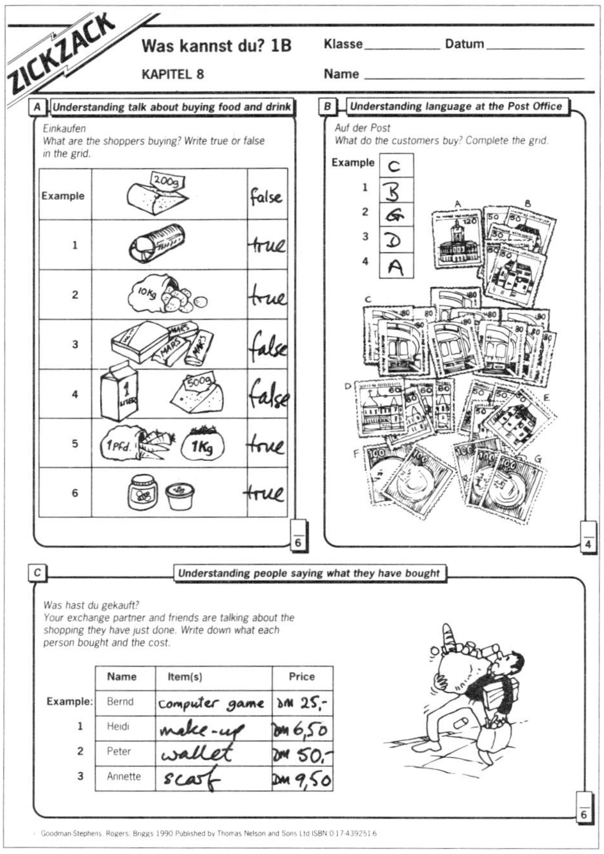

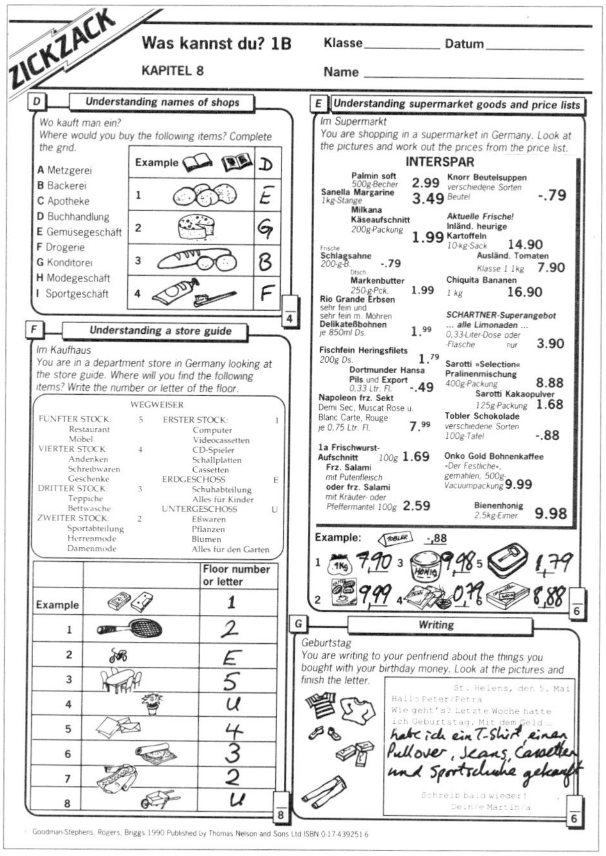

SPRECHEN

H Speaking

Tests ability to conduct shopping transactions. Three different sets of pairwork materials. Two activities per pupil in pairwork.
Pupils should be given one of the roles and should then work either with a partner or with the teacher (see Introduction).

Marking scheme:
2 marks per item up to a maximum of 10

1A ein Kilo Tomaten **2**
eineTube Mayonnaise **2**
eine Dose Cola **2**
eine Schachtel Pralinen/Schokoladen **2**
eine Packung Kaffee **2**
Was kostet/macht das? **2**
Total: **10** (maximum)

1B eine Packung Kekse **2**
einen Becher/eine Packung Butter **2**
250 Gramm Käse **2**
eine Flasche Apfelsaft**2**
ein Stück Seife **2**
Was kostet/macht das? **2**
Total: **10** (maximum)

2A zwei Stück Seife **2**
einen Riegel Mars/Marsriegel **2**
300 Gramm Wurst **2**
eine Kiste/8 Flaschen Bier **2**
eine Tube Zahnpasta **2**
Was kostet/macht das? **2**
Total: **10** (maximum)

2B einen Liter Milch **2**
einen Becher Margarine **2**
eine Tüte Gummibärchen **2**
ein Glas Marmelade **2**
eine Dose Suppe **2**
Was kostet/macht das? **2**
Total: **10** (maximum)

3A ein Glas Honig **2**
ein Pfund Karotten **2**
eine Flasche Cola **2**
eine Tüte/Packung Chips **2**
eine Schachtel Pralinen/Schokoladen **2**
Was kostet/macht das? **2**
Total: **10** (maximum)

3B einen Liter/eine Flasche Wein **2**
10 Kilo Kartoffeln **2**
eine Dose Heringe **2**
eine Flasche Limo(nade) **2**
eine Packung Kaffee **2**
Was kostet/macht das? **2**
Total: **10** (maximum)

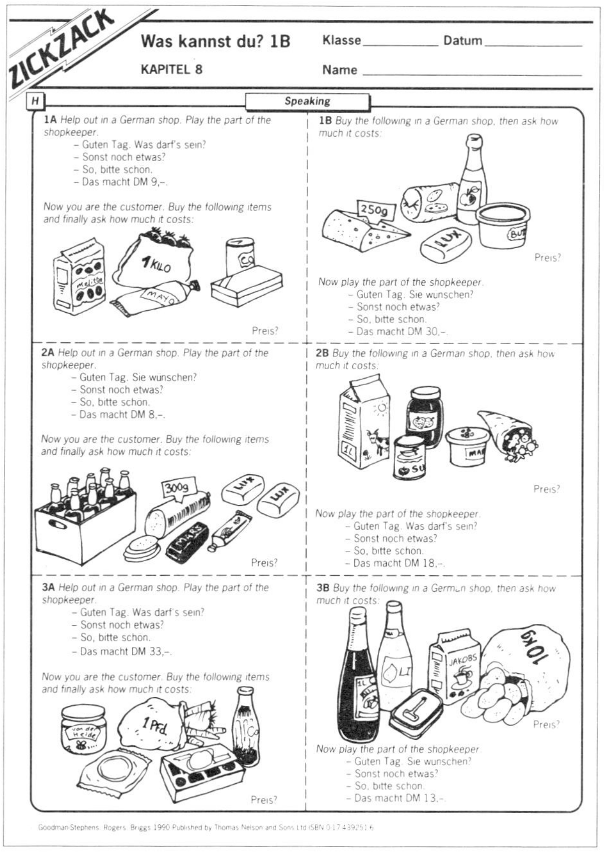
ZICKZACK

Was kannst du? 1B Klasse ________ Datum ________

KAPITEL 8 Name ________

H **Speaking**

1A *Help out in a German shop. Play the part of the shopkeeper.*
- Guten Tag. Was darf's sein?
- Sonst noch etwas?
- So, bitte schon.
- Das macht DM 9,–.

Now you are the customer. Buy the following items and finally ask how much it costs:

Preis?

1B *Buy the following in a German shop, then ask how much it costs:*

Preis?

Now play the part of the shopkeeper.
- Guten Tag. Sie wunschen?
- Sonst noch etwas?
- So, bitte schon.
- Das macht DM 30,–.

2A *Help out in a German shop. Play the part of the shopkeeper.*
- Guten Tag. Sie wünschen?
- Sonst noch etwas?
- So, bitte schon.
- Das macht DM 8,–.

Now you are the customer. Buy the following items and finally ask how much it costs:

Preis?

2B *Buy the following in a German shop, then ask how much it costs:*

Preis?

Now play the part of the shopkeeper.
- Guten Tag. Was darf's sein?
- Sonst noch etwas?
- So, bitte schon.
- Das macht DM 18,–.

3A *Help out in a German shop. Play the part of the shopkeeper.*
- Guten Tag. Was darf's sein?
- Sonst noch etwas?
- So, bitte schon.
- Das macht DM 33,–.

Now you are the customer. Buy the following items and finally ask how much it costs:

Preis?

3B *Buy the following in a German shop, then ask how much it costs:*

Preis?

Now play the part of the shopkeeper.
- Guten Tag. Sie wunschen?
- Sonst noch etwas?
- So, bitte schon.
- Das macht DM 13,–.

Goodman-Stephens, Rogers, Briggs 1990 Published by Thomas Nelson and Sons Ltd ISBN 0-17-439251-6

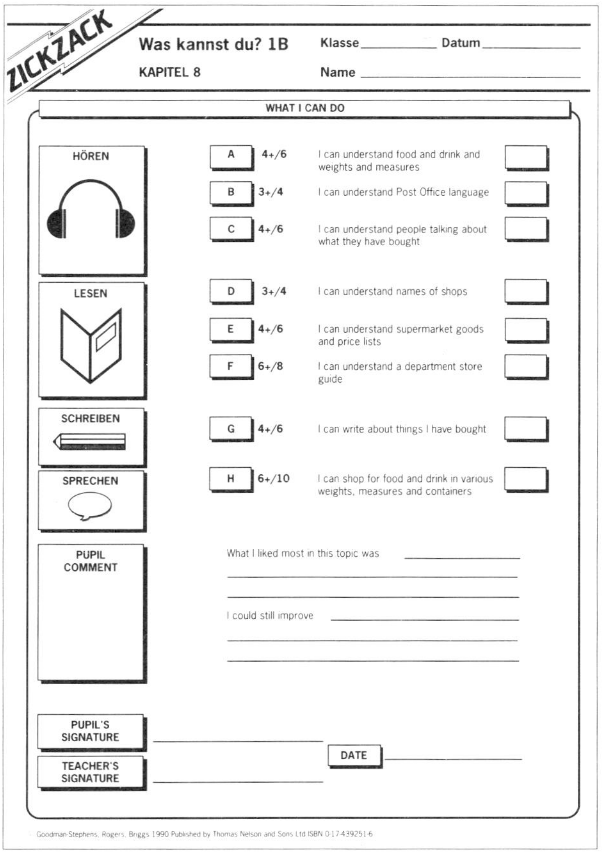
ZICKZACK

Was kannst du? 1B Klasse ________ Datum ________

KAPITEL 8 Name ________

WHAT I CAN DO

HÖREN	A	4+/6	I can understand food and drink and weights and measures	
	B	3+/4	I can understand Post Office language	
	C	4+/6	I can understand people talking about what they have bought	
LESEN	D	3+/4	I can understand names of shops	
	E	4+/6	I can understand supermarket goods and price lists	
	F	6+/8	I can understand a department store guide	
SCHREIBEN	G	4+/6	I can write about things I have bought	
SPRECHEN	H	6+/10	I can shop for food and drink in various weights, measures and containers	

PUPIL COMMENT

What I liked most in this topic was ________

I could still improve ________

PUPIL'S SIGNATURE ________

TEACHER'S SIGNATURE ________

DATE ________

Goodman-Stephens, Rogers, Briggs 1990 Published by Thomas Nelson and Sons Ltd ISBN 0-17-439251-6

Kapitel 9

HÖREN

A Understanding means of travel

Tests comprehension of modes of travel.

Wie kommst du zum Jugendklub?

Beispiel:
– Wie kommst du zum Jugendklub?
– Ich fahre mit dem Bus. Mein Fahrrad ist kaputt.

1 – Am Wochenende muß ich nach Bonn.
– Nach Bonn? So weit? Fährst du mit dem Mofa?
– Nein – mit der Bahn.
2 – Fliegst du nach England?
– Nein, ich fahre mit dem Zug und mit der Fähre.
3 – Kommst du mit in die Disco?
– Gern. Gehen wir zu Fuß?
– Lieber nicht. Das ist zu weit. Mein Vater bringt uns mit dem Wagen.
4 – Du kommst morgen mit der Straßenbahn zur Schule, oder?
– Nein, mit dem Moped. Das geht viel schneller.

Solution:
1H **2**H,C **3**E **4**B
Total: **5**

B Understanding language on stations and in trains

Tests comprehension of railway announcements and language used by railway officials and other passengers.

Bitte zurücktreten

Beispiel:
– Bitte zurücktreten

1 – In wenigen Minuten kommen wir in Köln an.
2 – Der Intercity-Zug nach Frankfurt hat fünf Minuten Verspätung.
3 – Sie haben Ihre Fahrkarte nicht entwertet.
4 – Ist noch jemand zugestiegen?
5 – Sie müssen in Augsburg umsteigen.

Solution:
1H **2**F **3**E **4**C **5**B
Total: **5**

C Understanding buying rail tickets

Tests comprehension of buying tickets.

Einmal nach Kiel

Beispiel:
– Einmal nach Kiel.
– Einfach?
– Nein, hin und zurück.
– DM 15,-.

1 – Zweimal nach Bonn.
– Einfach oder hin und zurück?
– Einfach.
– Also ... zweimal einfach nach Bonn. DM 26,-.
– Danke schön.
– Bitte schön.
2 – Dreimal nach Frankfurt, hin und zurück.
– Bitte schön. DM 42,-.

Solution:
1 2 single, DM 26,- **2** 3 return, DM 42,-
Total: **6**

D Understanding people planning a journey

Tests comprehension of people planning a journey.

Wie fahren wir dahin?

– Ich glaube, am besten fahren wir mit dem Taxi zum Flughafen.
– Nein, das kostet zu viel. Fahren wir mit dem Bus.
– Aber nein, wir haben zu viel Gepäck. Fahren wir lieber mit dem Wagen. Wir finden einen Parkplatz am Flughafen.
– OK.

– Fliegen wir Lufthansa?
– Nein, das ist zu teuer. Wir fliegen mit Charter.
– Ach so ...
– Und wie kommen wir vom Flughafen in Malaga nach Fuengirola?
– Hoffentlich mit dem Taxi ...
– Oder mit dem Bus. Was meinst du?
– Ach was. So weit ist es nicht. Ich glaube, am besten fahren wir mit dem Taxi dorthin. Das kostet nur DM 40,- oder so.
– Na ja. Machen wir das so.
– Gut. Und wo liegt das Hotel in Fuengirola?
– Direkt am Strand. Das ist nur zwei Minuten zu Fuß.
– Und wie kommen wir in die Stadt? Auch zu Fuß?
– Nein, ein Zug fährt alle zwanzig Minuten in die Stadtmitte.
– Das ist ganz praktisch.
– Ja, und billig.
– Toll.

Solution:
1B **2**C **3**B **4**A
Total: **4**

LESEN

E Understanding station signs and notices

Tests comprehension of signs and notices on stations and in trains.

Solution:
1F **2**H **3**I **4**B **5**D **6**C **7**G
Total: **7**

F Understanding information about cheaper rail fares

Tests comprehension of Inter-Rail card concessionary ticket information.

Solution:
1 DM 440; 1 month **(2)**
2 25/under 26
3 half
4 bus/ship or ferry/private railway **(any 2)**
5 DM 10 (refund)
Total: **7**

SCHREIBEN

G Writing

Tests pupils' ability to write about a delayed trip, giving a reason.

Marking scheme:
1 mark per item for communication, even with error, up to a maximum of 6.
der Zug / hatte / Verspätung / (und) die Reise / war / furchtbar/mies/fürchterlich/nicht gut
Total: **6**

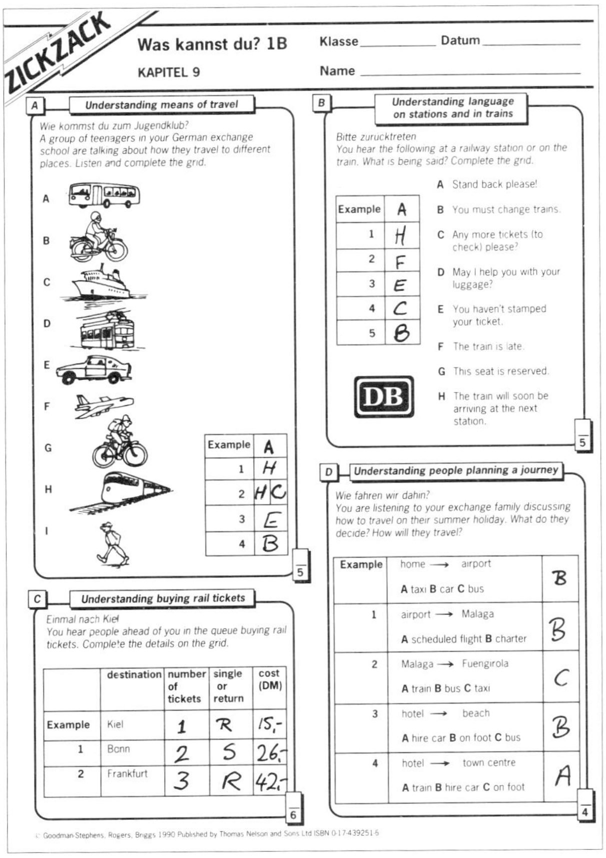

ZICKZACK **Was kannst du? 1B** Klasse ______ Datum ______
KAPITEL 9 Name ______

A Understanding means of travel

Wie kommst du zum Jugendklub?
A group of teenagers in your German exchange school are talking about how they travel to different places. Listen and complete the grid.

A B C D E F G H I

Example	A
1	H
2	H C
3	E
4	B

5

B Understanding language on stations and in trains

Bitte zurücktreten
You hear the following at a railway station or on the train. What is being said? Complete the grid.

Example	A
1	H
2	F
3	E
4	C
5	B

A Stand back please!
B You must change trains.
C Any more tickets (to check) please?
D May I help you with your luggage?
E You haven't stamped your ticket.
F The train is late.
G This seat is reserved.
H The train will soon be arriving at the next station.

DB

5

C Understanding buying rail tickets

Einmal nach Kiel
You hear people ahead of you in the queue buying rail tickets. Complete the details on the grid.

	destination	number of tickets	single or return	cost (DM)
Example	Kiel	1	R	15,-
1	Bonn	2	S	26,-
2	Frankfurt	3	R	42,-

6

D Understanding people planning a journey

Wie fahren wir dahin?
You are listening to your exchange family discussing how to travel on their summer holiday. What do they decide? How will they travel?

Example	home → airport **A** taxi **B** car **C** bus	B
1	airport → Malaga **A** scheduled flight **B** charter	B
2	Malaga → Fuengirola **A** train **B** bus **C** taxi	C
3	hotel → beach **A** hire car **B** on foot **C** bus	B
4	hotel → town centre **A** train **B** hire car **C** on foot	A

4

© Goodman-Stephens, Rogers, Briggs 1990 Published by Thomas Nelson and Sons Ltd ISBN 0-17-439251-6

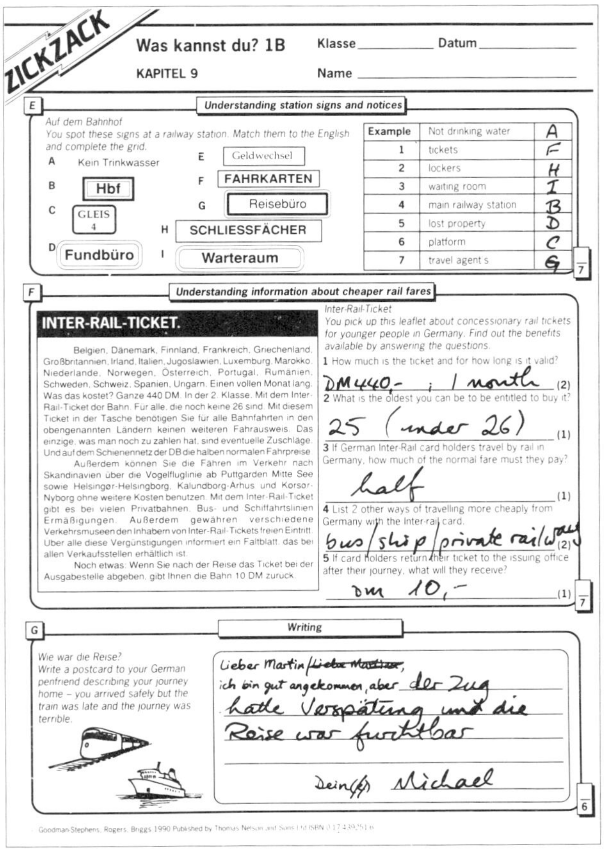

ZICKZACK **Was kannst du? 1B** Klasse ______ Datum ______
KAPITEL 9 Name ______

E Understanding station signs and notices

Auf dem Bahnhof
You spot these signs at a railway station. Match them to the English and complete the grid.

A Kein Trinkwasser
B Hbf
C GLEIS 4
D Fundbüro
E Geldwechsel
F FAHRKARTEN
G Reisebüro
H SCHLIESSFÄCHER
I Warteraum

Example	Not drinking water	A
1	tickets	F
2	lockers	H
3	waiting room	I
4	main railway station	B
5	lost property	D
6	platform	C
7	travel agent's	G

7

F Understanding information about cheaper rail fares

INTER-RAIL-TICKET.

Belgien, Dänemark, Finnland, Frankreich, Griechenland, Großbritannien, Irland, Italien, Jugoslawien, Luxemburg, Marokko, Niederlande, Norwegen, Österreich, Portugal, Rumänien, Schweden, Schweiz, Spanien, Ungarn. Einen vollen Monat lang. Was das kostet? Ganze 440 DM. In der 2. Klasse. Mit dem Inter-Rail-Ticket der Bahn. Für alle, die noch keine 26 sind. Mit diesem Ticket in der Tasche benötigen Sie für alle Bahnfahrten in den obengenannten Ländern keinen weiteren Fahrausweis. Das einzige, was man noch zu zahlen hat, sind eventuelle Zuschläge. Und auf dem Schienennetz der DB die halben normalen Fahrpreise.

Außerdem können Sie die Fähren im Verkehr nach Skandinavien über die Vogelfluglinie ab Puttgarden Mitte See sowie Helsingør-Helsingborg, Kalundborg-Århus und Korsør-Nyborg ohne weitere Kosten benutzen. Mit dem Inter-Rail-Ticket gibt es bei vielen Privatbahnen, Bus- und Schiffahrtslinien Ermäßigungen. Außerdem gewähren verschiedene Verkehrsmuseen den Inhabern von Inter-Rail-Tickets freien Eintritt. Über alle diese Vergünstigungen informiert ein Faltblatt, das bei allen Verkaufsstellen erhältlich ist.

Noch etwas: Wenn Sie nach der Reise das Ticket bei der Ausgabestelle abgeben, gibt Ihnen die Bahn 10 DM zurück.

Inter-Rail-Ticket
You pick up this leaflet about concessionary rail tickets for younger people in Germany. Find out the benefits available by answering the questions.

1 How much is the ticket and for how long is it valid?
DM 440,- ; 1 month (2)
2 What is the oldest you can be to be entitled to buy it?
25 (under 26) (1)
3 If German Inter-Rail card holders travel by rail in Germany, how much of the normal fare must they pay?
half (1)
4 List 2 other ways of travelling more cheaply from Germany with the Inter-rail card.
bus/ship/private railway (2)
5 If card holders return their ticket to the issuing office after their journey, what will they receive?
DM 10,- (1)

7

G Writing

Wie war die Reise?
Write a postcard to your German penfriend describing your journey home – you arrived safely but the train was late and the journey was terrible.

Lieber Martin/~~Liebe Martina~~,
ich bin gut angekommen, aber der Zug hatte Verspätung und die Reise war furchtbar

Dein(e) Michael

6

© Goodman-Stephens, Rogers, Briggs 1990 Published by Thomas Nelson and Sons Ltd ISBN 0-17-439251-6

SPRECHEN

H Speaking

Tests ability to find out and give travel information.
Three different sets of pairwork materials. Two activities per pupil in pairwork.
Pupils should be given one of the roles and should then work either with a partner or with the teacher (see Introduction).

Marking scheme:
1 mark per item up to a maximum of 10

1A Einmal (eine Fahrkarte) /einfach / nach Koblenz./ Wann (um wieviel Uhr) / fährt der Zug ab? / Von welchem Gleis (fährt der Zug)? / Einfach oder / hin und zurück? / Das kostet (macht) 30 Mark. / Um 19.20 (7.20) Uhr. / Von Gleis 2.
Total: **10** (maximum)

1B Einfach oder / hin und zurück? / Das kostet (macht) 25 Mark. / Um 21.30 (9.30) Uhr. / Von Gleis 4. /
Zweimal (zwei Fahrkarten) / nach Hamburg / hin und zurück./ Wann (um wieviel Uhr) / fährt der Zug ab? / Von welchem Gleis (fährt der Zug)?
Total: **10** (maximum)

2A Einmal (eine Fahrkarte) / nach Frankfurt / hin und zurück./ Wann (um wieviel Uhr) / fährt der Zug ab? / Von welchem Gleis (fährt der Zug)? /
Einfach oder / hin und zurück? / Das kostet (macht) 50 Mark. /Um 11.10 Uhr./Von Gleis 5.
Total: **10** (maximum)

2B Einfach oder / hin und zurück? / Das kostet (macht) 40 Mark. / Um 10.15 Uhr. / Von Gleis 3./
Dreimal (drei Fahrkarten) / einfach /nach Hannover./ Wann (um wieviel Uhr) / fährt der Zug ab? / Von welchem Gleis (fährt der Zug)?
Total: **10** (maximum)

3A Zweimal (zwei Fahrkarten) /einfach / nach Lübeck./ Wann (um wieviel Uhr) / fährt der Zug ab? / Von welchem Gleis (fährt der Zug)? /
Einfach oder / hin und zurück? / Das kostet (macht) 35 Mark. / Um 8.45 Uhr. /Von Gleis 5.
Total: **10** (maximum)

3B Einfach oder / hin und zurück? / Das kostet (macht) 20 Mark. / Um 22.00 (10.00) Uhr. / Von Gleis 1.
Einmal (eine Fahrkarte) / nach Köln / hin und zurück./ Wann (um wieviel Uhr) / fährt der Zug ab? / Von welchem Gleis (fährt der Zug)?
Total: **10** (maximum)

ZICKZACK

Was kannst du? 1B Klasse ______ Datum ______

KAPITEL 9 Name ______

H *Speaking*

1A *Ask for a single rail ticket to Koblenz and find out the departure time and platform.*

Koblenz →

?

GLEIS ?

Now you're the ticket seller. Ask if the customer wants a single or return, then state the cost and give the time of departure and platform when asked.

→ oder ↔ ? 19:20

DM 30,- Gl. 2

1B *Play the part of a ticket seller at a station. Ask if the customer wants single or return, then state the cost and, when asked, give departure time and platform.*

→ oder ↔ ? 21:30

DM 25,- Gl. 4

Now you're the customer. You want 2 return tickets to Hamburg. Find out the departure time and platform.

Hamburg ↔

?

GLEIS ?

2A *Ask for a return rail ticket to Frankfurt and find out the departure time and platform.*

Frankfurt ↔

?

GLEIS ?

Now you're the ticket seller. Ask if the customer wants a single or return, then state the cost and give departure time and platform.

→ oder ↔ ? 11:10

DM 50,- Gl. 5

2B *Play the part of a ticket seller at a station. Ask if the customer wants single or return, then state the cost and, when asked, give departure time and platform.*

→ oder ↔ ? 10:15

DM 40,- Gl. 3

Now you're the customer. You want 3 single tickets to Hanover. Find out the departure time and platform.

Hannover →

?

GLEIS ?

3A *Ask for two single rail tickets to Lübeck and find out the departure time and platform.*

Lübeck →

?

GLEIS ?

Now you're the ticket seller. Ask if the customer wants a single or return, then state the cost and give departure time and platform.

→ oder ↔ ? 08:45

DM 35,- Gl. 5

3B *Play the part of a ticket seller at a station. Ask if the customer wants single or return, then state the cost and, when asked, give departure time and platform.*

→ oder ↔ ? 22:00

DM 20,- Gl. 1

Now you're the customer. You want a return ticket to Cologne. Find out the departure time and platform.

Köln ↔

?

GLEIS ?

© Goodman-Stephens, Rogers, Briggs 1990 Published by Thomas Nelson and Sons Ltd ISBN 0-17-439251-6

ZICKZACK

Was kannst du? 1B Klasse ______ Datum ______

KAPITEL 9 Name ______

WHAT I CAN DO

HÖREN	A	4+/5	I can understand people talking about different ways to travel	☐
	B	3+/5	I can understand railway announcements and questions and requests on trains	☐
	C	4+/6	I can understand people buying rail tickets	☐
	D	3+/4	I can understand people talking about a journey	☐
LESEN	E	5+/7	I can understand railway signs and notices	☐
	F	5+/7	I can understand information about reduced price tickets	☐
SCHREIBEN	G	4+/6	I can write simple details about a journey	☐
SPRECHEN	H	6+/10	I can buy rail tickets and answer questions about train times and platforms	☐

PUPIL COMMENT

What I liked most in this topic was ______

I could still improve ______

PUPIL'S SIGNATURE ______

TEACHER'S SIGNATURE ______ DATE ______

Goodman-Stephens, Rogers, Briggs 1990 Published by Thomas Nelson and Sons Ltd ISBN 0-17-439251-6

Attainment Test
Kapitel 7-9

HÖREN

A Understanding questions and answers

Tests gist comprehension of transactional language in chapters 7-9.

Entschuldigung

1 – Entschuldigung, wo ist hier die Schuhabteilung?
– Im dritten Stock, sehen Sie?
– Ach ja, vielen Dank.
– Nichts zu danken.
2 – Entschuldigung ... ich suche den Dom.
– Den Dom? Zweite Straße links 'rein.
– Danke schön.
– Bitte schön.
3 – Was gibt es hier zu sehen?
– Das Schloß, das alte Rathaus und ... ja, die Stadtmauer.
4 – Seite 45 ... Du da hinten. Hör zu.
5 – Bitte schön?
– Zwei Briefmarken zu achtzig Pfennig.
– DM 1,60. Bitte schön.
– Danke.
6 – Guten Tag.
– Guten Tag ... einmal einfach nach Köln.
– DM 15,50.
7 – Ich habe ein paar Geschenke mitgebracht ... Das ist für Sie, Frau Schmidt.
– Für mich? Vielen Dank.
– Und das ist für Sie, Herr Schmidt.
– Das ist aber nett von dir.
8 – Entschuldigung. Ist hier ein Parkplatz in der Nähe?
– Ja, gleich hier um die Ecke.

Solution:
1E **2**G **3**F **4**C **5**H **6**J **7**D **8**B
Total: **8**

B Understanding questions

Tests gist comprehension of questions across all three chapters.

Das ist die Frage

1 – Entschuldigung. Wo ist der Bahnhof?
2 – Ist das weit von hier?
3 – Was kann ich heute nachmittag machen?
4 – Sonst noch etwas?
5 – Wo kann ich hier Cassetten bekommen?
6 – Was kostet ein Brief nach Amerika?
7 – Wo warst du?
8 – Was hast du bei Hertie gekauft?
9 – Wie kommst du zur Schule?

Solution:
1C **2**B **3**A **4**A **5**C **6**B **7**C **8**C **9**B
Total: **9**

C Understanding information given in a department store

Tests detailed comprehension of conversations and announcements heard in a department store.

Im Kaufhaus

1 – Darf ich Ihnen helfen?
– Ja, ähm, kann ich hier Schreibpapier bekommen?
– Nein, hier nicht. Das finden Sie im Untergeschoß.
– Danke schön.
2 – Bitte schön?
– Guten Tag. Ich hätte gern ... ich suche Sportschuhe für meine Tochter. Ist das hier in diesem Stock?
– Ja, dort drüben, sehen Sie?
– Ach ja, danke.
– Nichts zu danken.
3 – Kann ich behilflich sein?
– Ja, hoffentlich. Ich möchte mir einen Schal kaufen.
– Ja, die Schals sind im vierten Stock. Hier müssen Sie nach oben ... die Treppe da in der Ecke.
– Vielen Dank.
4 – ... und im zweiten Stock gibt es alles für den Schulbeginn: Notizblöcke, Lineale, Bleistifte, Kulis, Radiergummis und so weiter. Sie finden einfach alles. Das nimmt kein Ende!

Solution:
1a writing paper (stationery)
b basement
2a sports shoes (trainers)
b over there (on the same floor)
3a scarf
b fourth floor (up the stairs)
4 B, D, H
Total: **9**

D Understanding details of journeys

Tests detailed comprehension of means of travel, both in the future and in the past.

Unterwegs

– Wann fährst du nach Italien?
– Im August. Wir fliegen mit einem Charterflug nach Rom.
– Ist das billig?
– Ja, der Flug kostet nur DM 300,- pro Person.
– Wie lange dauert der Flug?
– Ich weiß nicht genau, ich glaube so ungefähr zwei Stunden. Und vom Flugplatz fahren wir direkt mit dem Bus in die Stadtmitte zu unserem Hotel ...
– Wir sind letztes Jahr auch nach Rom gefahren.
– Mit der Bahn?

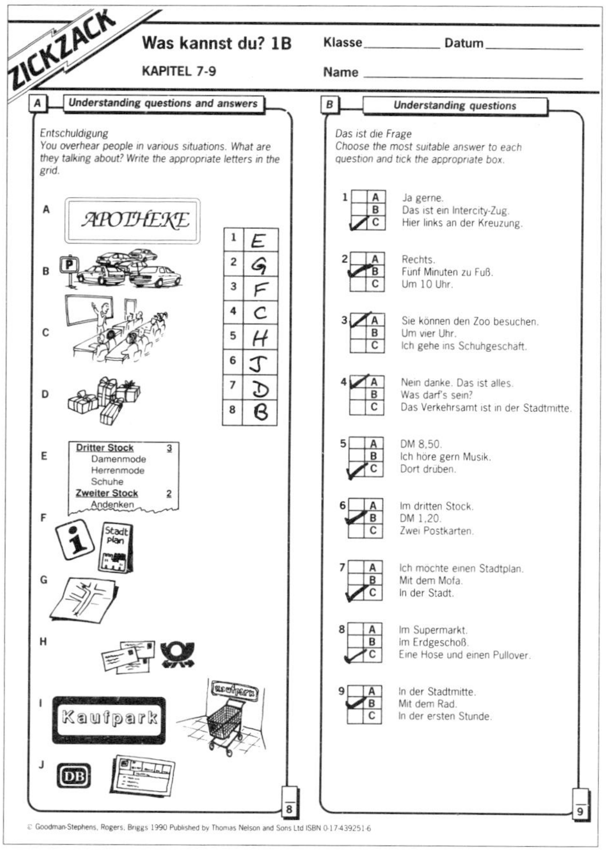

ZICKZACK **Was kannst du? 1B** Klasse ________ Datum ________
KAPITEL 7-9 Name ________________

A Understanding questions and answers

Entschuldigung
You overhear people in various situations. What are they talking about? Write the appropriate letters in the grid.

1	E
2	G
3	F
4	C
5	H
6	J
7	D
8	B

8

B Understanding questions

Das ist die Frage
Choose the most suitable answer to each question and tick the appropriate box.

1 A Ja gerne. B Das ist ein Intercity-Zug. C ✓ Hier links an der Kreuzung.
2 A Rechts. B ✓ Fünf Minuten zu Fuß. C Um 10 Uhr.
3 A ✓ Sie können den Zoo besuchen. B Um vier Uhr. C Ich gehe ins Schuhgeschaft.
4 A ✓ Nein danke. Das ist alles. B Was darf's sein? C Das Verkehrsamt ist in der Stadtmitte.
5 A DM 8,50. B Ich höre gern Musik. C ✓ Dort drüben.
6 A Im dritten Stock. B ✓ DM 1,20. C Zwei Postkarten.
7 A Ich möchte einen Stadtplan. B Mit dem Mofa. C ✓ In der Stadt.
8 A Im Supermarkt. B Im Erdgeschoß. C ✓ Eine Hose und einen Pullover.
9 A In der Stadtmitte. B ✓ Mit dem Rad. C In der ersten Stunde.

9

© Goodman-Stephens, Rogers, Briggs 1990 Published by Thomas Nelson and Sons Ltd ISBN 0-17-439251-6

– Nee, mit dem Auto. Das war im Juli. Es war so heiß! Wir sind Autobahn gefahren, aber es hat trotzdem sehr lange gedauert - über fünfzehn Stunden!
– Mensch, das war ziemlich lang.
– Und wie! ... und teuer ... wir mußten auch für die Autobahn bezahlen.

Solution:
1 Italy (Rome)
2 in August
3 by plane (Charter)
4 DM 300,-
5 (about) two hours
6 by bus
7 by car
8 (over) fifteen hours
9 had to pay (to use it)
Total: **9**

LESEN

E Understanding the price list for a ferry crossing

Tests comprehension of a price list for a ferry crossing.

Solution:
1 DM 2,30 **2** DM 2,30 **3** DM 4,50 **4** DM 3,50
Total: **4**

F Understanding general information about a town

Tests comprehension of facts and figures about Berlin.

Solution:
1H **2**O **3**J **4**G **5**K **6**D **7**E **8**M **9**L **10**I
Total: **10**

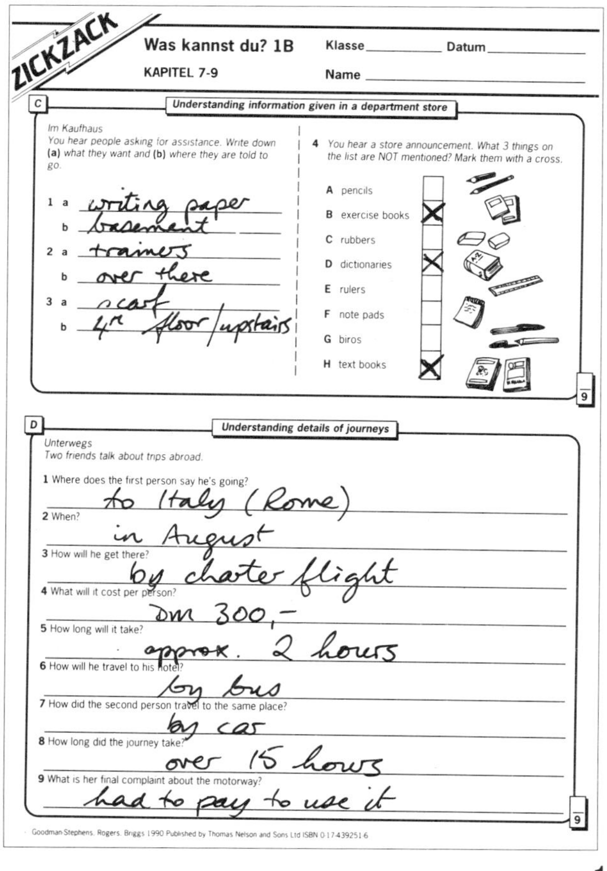

ZICKZACK **Was kannst du? 1B** Klasse ________ Datum ________
KAPITEL 7-9 Name ________________

C Understanding information given in a department store

Im Kaufhaus
*You hear people asking for assistance. Write down **(a)** what they want and **(b)** where they are told to go.*

1 a writing paper
b basement
2 a trainers
b over there
3 a scarf
b 4th floor/upstairs

4 *You hear a store announcement. What 3 things on the list are NOT mentioned? Mark them with a cross.*

A pencils
B exercise books ☒
C rubbers
D dictionaries ☒
E rulers
F note pads
G biros
H text books ☒

9

D Understanding details of journeys

Unterwegs
Two friends talk about trips abroad.

1 Where does the first person say he's going?
to Italy (Rome)
2 When?
in August
3 How will he get there?
by charter flight
4 What will it cost per person?
DM 300,-
5 How long will it take?
approx. 2 hours
6 How will he travel to his hotel?
by bus
7 How did the second person travel to the same place?
by car
8 How long did the journey take?
over 15 hours
9 What is her final complaint about the motorway?
had to pay to use it

9

© Goodman-Stephens, Rogers, Briggs 1990 Published by Thomas Nelson and Sons Ltd ISBN 0-17-439251-6

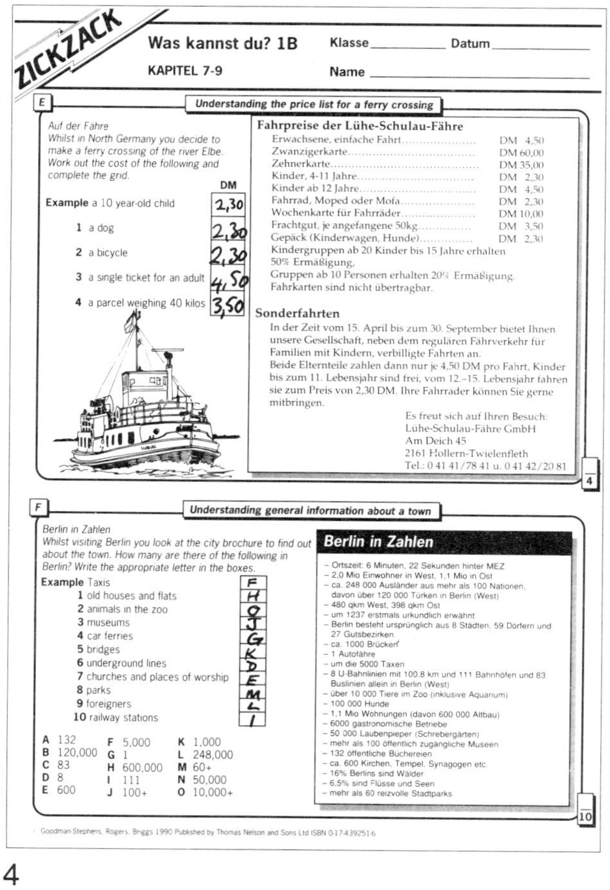

ZICKZACK **Was kannst du? 1B** Klasse ________ Datum ________
KAPITEL 7-9 Name ________________

E Understanding the price list for a ferry crossing

Auf der Fähre
Whilst in North Germany you decide to make a ferry crossing of the river Elbe. Work out the cost of the following and complete the grid.

	DM
Example a 10 year-old child	2,30
1 a dog	2,30
2 a bicycle	2,30
3 a single ticket for an adult	4,50
4 a parcel weighing 40 kilos	3,50

Fahrpreise der Lühe-Schulau-Fähre

Erwachsene, einfache Fahrt	DM 4,50
Zwanzigerkarte	DM 60,00
Zehnerkarte	DM 35,00
Kinder, 4-11 Jahre	DM 2,30
Kinder ab 12 Jahre	DM 4,50
Fahrrad, Moped oder Mofa	DM 2,30
Wochenkarte für Fahrräder	DM 10,00
Frachtgut, je angefangene 50kg	DM 3,50
Gepäck (Kinderwagen, Hunde)	DM 2,30

Kindergruppen ab 20 Kinder bis 15 Jahre erhalten 50% Ermäßigung,
Gruppen ab 10 Personen erhalten 20% Ermäßigung.
Fahrkarten sind nicht übertragbar.

Sonderfahrten
In der Zeit vom 15. April bis zum 30. September bietet Ihnen unsere Gesellschaft, neben dem regulären Fährverkehr für Familien mit Kindern, verbilligte Fahrten an.
Beide Elternteile zahlen dann nur je 4,50 DM pro Fahrt, Kinder bis zum 11. Lebensjahr sind frei, vom 12.-15. Lebensjahr fahren sie zum Preis von 2,30 DM. Ihre Fahrräder können Sie gerne mitbringen.

Es freut sich auf Ihren Besuch:
Lühe-Schulau-Fähre GmbH
Am Deich 45
2161 Hollern-Twielenfleth
Tel.: 0 41 41/78 41 u. 0 41 42/20 81

4

F Understanding general information about a town

Berlin in Zahlen
Whilst visiting Berlin you look at the city brochure to find out about the town. How many are there of the following in Berlin? Write the appropriate letter in the boxes.

Example Taxis	F
1 old houses and flats	H
2 animals in the zoo	O
3 museums	J
4 car ferries	G
5 bridges	K
6 underground lines	D
7 churches and places of worship	E
8 parks	M
9 foreigners	L
10 railway stations	I

A 132	**F** 5,000	**K** 1,000
B 120,000	**G** 1	**L** 248,000
C 83	**H** 600,000	**M** 60+
D 8	**I** 111	**N** 50,000
E 600	**J** 100+	**O** 10,000+

Berlin in Zahlen
- Ortszeit: 6 Minuten, 22 Sekunden hinter MEZ
- 2,0 Mio Einwohner in West, 1,1 Mio in Ost
- ca. 248 000 Ausländer aus mehr als 100 Nationen, davon über 120 000 Türken in Berlin (West)
- 480 qkm West, 398 qkm Ost
- um 1237 erstmals urkundlich erwähnt
- Berlin besteht ursprünglich aus 8 Städten, 59 Dörfern und 27 Gutsbezirken
- ca. 1000 Brücken
- 1 Autofähre
- um die 5000 Taxen
- 8 U-Bahnlinien mit 100,8 km und 111 Bahnhöfen und 83 Buslinien allein in Berlin (West)
- über 10 000 Tiere im Zoo (inklusive Aquarium)
- 100 000 Hunde
- 1,1 Mio Wohnungen (davon 600 000 Altbau)
- 6000 gastronomische Betriebe
- 50 000 Laubenpieper (Schrebergärten)
- mehr als 100 öffentlich zugängliche Museen
- 132 öffentliche Büchereien
- ca. 600 Kirchen, Tempel, Synagogen etc.
- 16% Berlins sind Wälder
- 6,5% sind Flüsse und Seen
- mehr als 60 reizvolle Stadtparks

10

© Goodman-Stephens, Rogers, Briggs 1990 Published by Thomas Nelson and Sons Ltd ISBN 0-17-439251-6

G Understanding a town brochure about shopping hours

Tests comprehension of shopping hours in Berlin.

Solution:
1F **2**F **3**T **4**T **5**T **6**F **7**T
Total: **7**

H Understanding information about rail services

Tests comprehension of the services available from *Deutsche Bundesbahn.*

Solution:
A C D F
Total: **4**

SCHREIBEN

I Writing

Tests knowledge of food and drink vocabulary and weights, measures and containers.

Solution:
1 ein (1) Pfund / Tomaten
2 sechs (6) Tüten (Packungen) / Chips
3 zwei (2) Packungen / Kekse
4 drei (3) Flaschen / Limonade
5 fünf (5) Dosen / Cola
Total: **10**

J Writing

An open-ended activity which tests knowledge of travel and transport, town facilities, holiday activities and shopping.

Marking scheme:
Allow maximum of 2 marks per item of information requested up to a maximum total of 10.
where on holiday **(2)**
how travelled **(2)**
what the journey was like **(2)**
what there is to see in town **(2)**
what there is to do in town **(2)**
what was bought yesterday **(2)**
Total: **10** (maximum)

SPRECHEN

K Speaking

Tests ability to talk about leisure time activities, including travelling and times. Four different sets of pairwork materials. Pupils should be given one of the roles and should then work either with a partner or with the teacher (see Introduction).

Marking scheme:
1 mark per item of information up to a maximum of 15, plus a maximum of 5 discretionary marks for fluency, accuracy, idiom/elegance of expression etc.

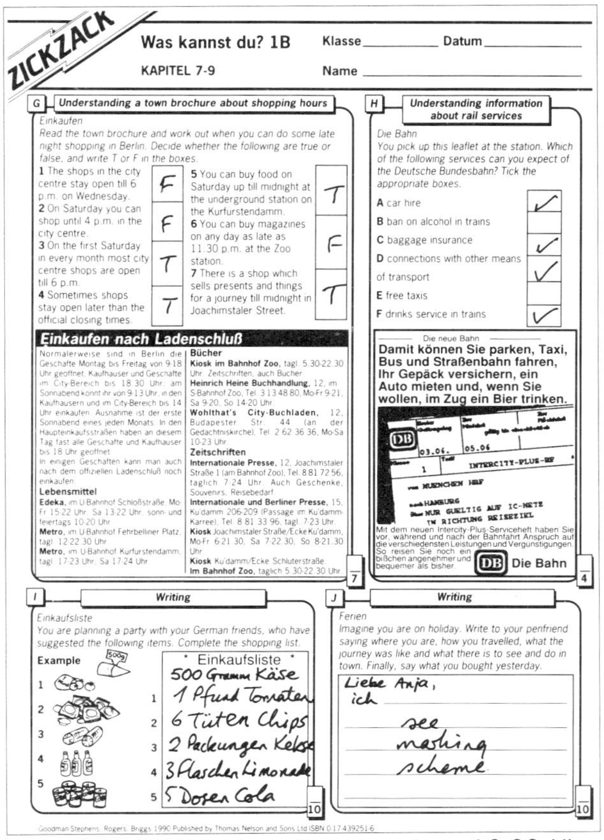

1A Ich fahre / am Samstag / um 12.00 Uhr / mit dem Bus / in die Stadt. / Das dauert / zwanzig Minuten. / Ich treffe mich / mit meinen Freunden (meinem Freund, meiner Freundin) / vor dem (am) Bahnhof. / Wir gehen in den Park / (und) wir spielen Tennis. / (Dann) gehen wir / ins Eiscafé. / Wir trinken / eine Cola / oder essen / ein Eis.
Total: **15** (maximum) **+5** (maximum) = **20**

1B Ich fahre / am Freitag / um 3 Uhr / mit dem Fahrrad / in die Stadt. / Das dauert / 15 Minuten. / Ich treffe mich / mit meinen Freunden (meinem Freund, meiner Freundin) / in der Hauptstraße. / Wir gehen / ins Kino / (oder) zum Popkonzert. / (Dann) gehen wir / ins Jugendzentrum / und (wir) hören Musik / oder spielen Tischtennis.
Total: **15** (maximum) **+5** (maximum) = **20**

2A Ich fahre / am Mittwoch / um 4 Uhr / mit dem Zug (der Bahn) / in die Stadt. / Das dauert / 30 Minuten. / Ich treffe mich / mit meinen Freunden / am Marktplatz. / Wir gehen schwimmen / (oder) (wir gehen) ins (zum) Sportzentrum / und spielen Basketball. / (Dann) gehen wir / ins Kino / oder in die (zur) Disco.
Total: **15** (maximum) **+5** (maximum) = **20**

2B Ich fahre / am Donnerstag / um 5 Uhr / mit der Straßenbahn / in die Stadt. / Das dauert / 25 Minuten. / Ich treffe mich / mit meinen Freunden / am (vor dem) Dom. / Wir gehen schwimmen. / (Dann) gehen wir / ins Café / und trinken Kaffee oder Cola, / (oder) (wir gehen) ins (zum) Jugendzentrum / und spielen Tischtennis.
Total: **15** (maximum) **+5** (maximum) = **20**

ZICKZACK

Was kannst du? 1B

KAPITEL 7-9

Klasse__________ Datum______________

Name ______________________________

K **Speaking**

1A *Talk to your partner about what you do in your free time: say*

when you go into town (day and time), Fr / Sa✓ / So 12:00

how you get there, → Stadt

how long it takes, 20 Min.

where you meet your friends, DB

what you do, STADTPARK

Dann Eiscafe

Then ask your partner what (s)he does in his/her free time.

1B *Ask your partner what (s)he does during his/her free time.*
Then tell your partner what you do yourself: say

when you go into town (day and time), Do / Fr✓ / Sa 15:00

how you get there, → Stadt

how long it takes, 15 Min.

where you meet your friends, HAUPTSTRASSE

what you do, KINO oder POPKONZERT Evi Bamm *Freitag*

Dann JUGENDZENTRUM oder

2A *Talk to your partner about what you do in your free time: say*

when you go into town (day and time), Di / Mi✓ / Do 16:00

how you get there, → Stadt

how long it takes, 30 Min.

where you meet your friends, MARKTPLATZ

what you do, oder

Dann KINO oder **Heiße Zeiten Disco**

Then ask your partner what (s)he does in his/her free time.

2B *Ask your partner what (s)he does during his/her free time.*
Then tell your partner what you do yourself: say

when you go into town (day and time), Mi / Do✓ / Fr 17:00

how you get there, → Stadt

how long it takes, 25 Min.

where you meet your friends, SCHWIMMHALLE

what you do,

Dann Café oder JUGENDZENTRUM

© Goodman-Stephens, Rogers, Briggs 1990 Published by Thomas Nelson and Sons Ltd ISBN 0-17-439251-6

ZICKZACK

Was kannst du? 1B

KAPITEL 7-9

Klasse__________ Datum______________

Name ______________________________

WHAT I CAN DO

HÖREN	A	6+/8	I can understand questions and answers about things in town, at home and at school	☐
	B	7+/9	I can understand questions about town, shopping, school and home	☐
	C	7+/9	I can understand information in a department store	☐
	D	7+/9	I can understand details of travelling	☐
LESEN	E	3+/4	I can understand a price list for ferry crossings	☐
	F	7+/10	I can understand general information about a town	☐
	G	5+/7	I can understand information about shopping hours	☐
	H	3+/4	I can understand information on a railways leaflet	☐
SCHREIBEN	I	7+/10	I can write a shopping list for basic food and drink	☐
	J	7+/10	I can write about a town and how I travelled there, and write about what I've bought	☐
SPRECHEN	K	14+/20	I can talk about my leisure time activities, including travelling and times	☐

PUPIL COMMENT

What I liked most in this topic was ______________________

I could still improve ______________________

PUPIL'S SIGNATURE ______________________

TEACHER'S SIGNATURE ______________________

DATE ______________________

© Goodman-Stephens, Rogers, Briggs 1990 Published by Thomas Nelson and Sons Ltd ISBN 0-17-439251-6

Kapitel 10

HÖREN

A Understanding dates and months

Tests comprehension of dates and months.

Wann?

Beispiel:
– Du, wann spielt der HSV gegen Stuttgart? Weißt du das?
– Ich weiß nicht. Ist das vielleicht im Juli?
– Moment mal, ich schau' nach ... ach ja, im Juli. Am zwölften.

1 – Anne, vergiß nicht ... am neunten März gibt's die Party bei Stefan.
– Ist das ein Freitag?
– Nein, ein Samstag.
2 – Silke, wann ist das Evi Bamm Konzert in Hannover?
– Am ersten Januar ... ja, am ersten Januar.
– Gehst du hin?
– Ja, na klar!
3 – Sag mal, Peter. Wann hast du eigentlich Geburtstag?
– Am elften Mai.
– Also nächsten Freitag?
– Ja.
– Gibst du eine Party?
– Ja, natürlich! Kommst du?
– Ja.

Solution:
1 9th March **2** 1st January **3** 11th May
Total: **6**

B Understanding reasons for turning down an invitation

Tests comprehension of excuses for declining invitations.

Tut mir leid

Beispiel:
– Hallo Holger.
– Hallo Sven.
– Du, am Samstag hab' ich Geburtstag und geb' eine Party. Kannst du kommen?
– Ja gern! Oh, Samstag sagst du? Ach nein, das geht nicht. Wir haben Besuch. Meine Kusine kommt fürs Wochenende.
– Naja ... Schade.

1 – He du, ich gehe heute ins Kino. Kommst du mit?
– Ich kann leider nicht. Ich gehe mit Sabine aus ... ins Eiscafé.
– Viel Spaß also!
– Danke.
2 – Dorit, hast du Lust, schwimmen zu gehen?
– Ja, wann denn?
– Morgen. Morgen abend so gegen sechs.
– Ach nein, das geht leider nicht. Morgen abend geh' ich zum Jugendzentrum. Ich treffe mich mit Freunden da.
– OK. Vielleicht ein anderes Mal.
– Ja, ja gut.
3 – Du, Bernd, hast du heute abend Zeit?
– Ja, wieso denn?
– Wir gehen alle Rollschuhlaufen. Kommst du mit?
– Nein, ich kann nicht ...
– Wieso nicht?
– Ich habe kein Geld, du.
– Oh Schade.

Solution:
1 1C **2** 3E **3** 6F
Total: **6**

C Understanding descriptions of people

Tests comprehension of personal descriptions

Wie sehen sie aus?

Beispiel:
Meine beste Freundin heißt Ruth. Sie hat kurze blonde Haare und trägt oft einen dunkelblauen Anorak und Jeans. Die ist wirklich toll!

1 Anke mag ich sehr. Sie hat lange blonde Haare und trägt eine Brille. Oft trägt sie ein weißes T-Shirt und eine schwarze Hose. Ich finde sie sehr sympathisch.
2 Guck mal. Hier auf dem Bild. Das ist Elizabeth. Die ist meine beste Freundin. Die hat, wie du siehst, schöne lange Haare - ganz schwarz. Die trägt immer einen schwarzen Rock und eine weiße Bluse.
3 Die Ute ist auch eine Freundin von mir. Sie hat kurze schwarze Haare und trägt eine Brille. Oft trägt sie eine schwarze Jacke mit einem gestreiften Pulli und eine schwarze Cordhose dazu.

Solution:
1 Anke **E**
2 Elizabeth **C**
3 Ute **B**
Total: **3**

D Understanding people talking about what they have done recently

Tests comprehension of activities people have been doing recently.

Freizeit

Beispiel:
– Petra, was hast du gestern abend gemacht?
– Gestern abend? Ich bin mit Kurt ins Kino gegangen. Der Film war wirklich gut. Der heißt *'Die Brücke'*.

1 – Und du, Michael, was hast du gestern gemacht?
– Nicht viel. Ich bin zu Hause geblieben und hab' Schularbeiten gemacht.
2 – Gestern war ich in der Stadt. Ich hab' dort ein paar Freunde getroffen, und wir haben zusammen Eis gegessen.

3 – Am Samstag bin ich zu einer Party gegangen ... bei Sonja. Das war wirklich toll. Ich hab' fast den ganzen Abend mit Raphael getanzt. Der ist wirklich sympathisch.
4 – Bist du gestern mit Konrad in die Disco gegangen?
– Nee, dazu hatte ich keine Lust. Ich bin zu Hause geblieben und hab' ein bißchen ferngesehen.
5 – Warum bist du am Freitag nicht in die Disco gegangen?
– Mensch, mir ging es so schlecht. Ich hatte die Grippe. Ich bin zu Hause geblieben und hab' mit meinem Bruder Karten gespielt.

Solution:
1C **2**B **3**D **4**F **5**E
Total: **5**

LESEN

E Understanding advertisements for sport and leisure

Tests comprehension of advertisements for sports and leisure facilities and opportunities.

Solution:
1E **2**C **3**D **4**G **5**F **6**B **7**A **8**I **9**H
Total: **9**

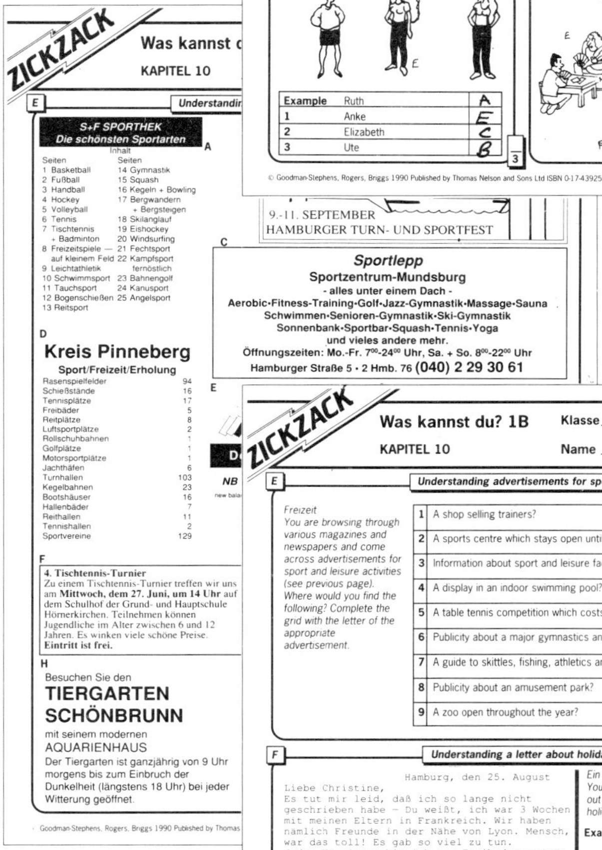

F Understanding a letter about holiday activities

Tests comprehension of a letter about holiday activities.

Solution:
any 5 from
- visited friends near Lyon
- went swimming (to the swimming pool, every morning)
- met a (nice) boy
- did lots together
- played table tennis
- went to the cinema
- watched TV
- went to (birthday) party
- danced (all evening)

Total: **5**

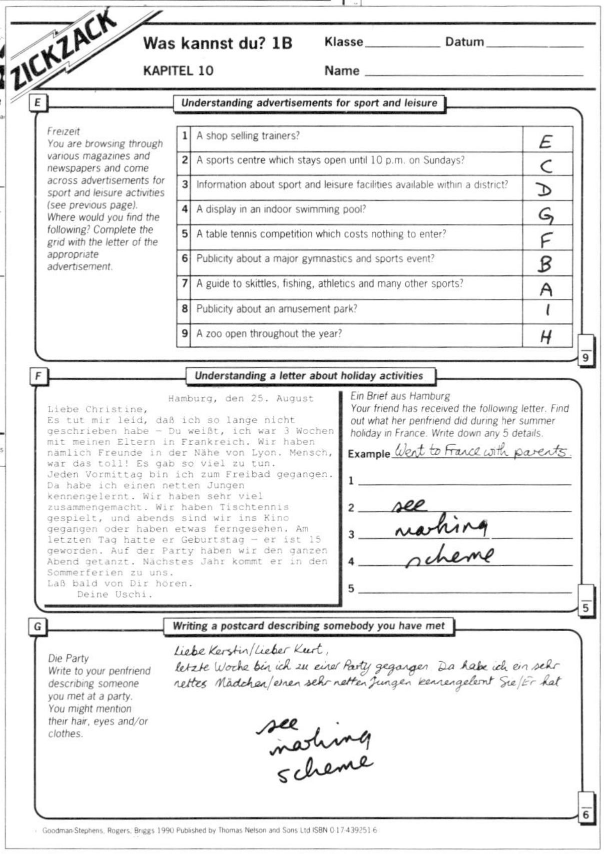

SCHREIBEN

G Writing a postcard describing somebody you have met

Tests ability to write short personal descriptions.

Solution:
6 details from
schöne/lange/kurze/blonde/schwarze Haare
blaue/graue/grüne/etc. Augen
trägt / eine Brille/eine Cordhose/einen Pulli/ etc.
Total: **6**

SPRECHEN

H Speaking

Tests ability to give out and receive invitations. Three different sets of pairwork materials. Two activities per pupil in pairwork.
Pupils should be given one of the roles and should then work either with a partner or with the teacher (see Introduction).

Marking scheme:
1 mark per item up to a maximum of 10

1A Ich gehe / (am) Samstag / auf eine Party. / Hast du Lust / mitzukommen? (Willst du / mitkommen?) / (Das (die Party) fängt) um 7 (Uhr an).
Ja, gerne. (Ich komme gerne mit.) / Wann (Um wieviel Uhr) / fängt das (der Film) an? (Wann treffen wir uns?)
Total: **10** (maximum)

1B Ja, gerne. (Ich komme gerne mit.) / Wann (Um wieviel Uhr) / fängt das (die Party) an? (Wann treffen wir uns?) /
Ich gehe / heute nachmittag / ins Kino. / Hast du Lust / mitzukommen? (Willst du / mitkommen?) / (Das (der Film) fängt) um 4 (Uhr an).
Total: **10** (maximum)

2A Ich gehe / (am) Freitag / in die (zu einer) Disco. / Hast du Lust / mitzukommen? (Willst du / mitkommen?) / (Das fängt) um 8 (Uhr an).
Ja, gerne. (Ich komme gerne mit.) / Wann (Um wieviel Uhr) / gehen wir? (Wann treffen wir uns?)
Total: **10** (maximum)

2B Ja, gerne. (Ich komme gerne mit.) / Wann (Um wieviel Uhr) / fängt das (die Disco) an? (Wann treffen wir uns?) /
Ich gehe / nächsten Donnerstag / schwimmen (zum Schwimmbad etc.). / Hast du Lust / mitzukommen? (Willst du / mitkommen?) / (Wir gehen / treffen uns) um 2 (Uhr).
Total: **10** (maximum)

3A Ich gehe / morgen / zu einem Fußballspiel (zum Stadion). / Hast du Lust / mitzukommen? (Willst du / mitkommen?) / (Das (Spiel) fängt) um 2 (Uhr an)./
Ja, gerne. (Ich komme gerne mit.) / Wann (Um wieviel Uhr) / fängt das (Spiel) an? (Wann treffen wir uns (spielen wir)?)
Total: **10** (maximum)

3B Ja, gerne. (Ich komme gerne mit.) / Wann (Um wieviel Uhr) / fängt das (Spiel) an? (Wann treffen wir uns?) /
Ich gehe / (am) Mittwoch / Tennis spielen. / Hast du Lust / mitzukommen? (Willst du / mitkommen?) / (Das (Spiel) fängt) um 5 (Uhr an). (Wir spielen (gehen) um 5 Uhr.)
Total: **10** (maximum)

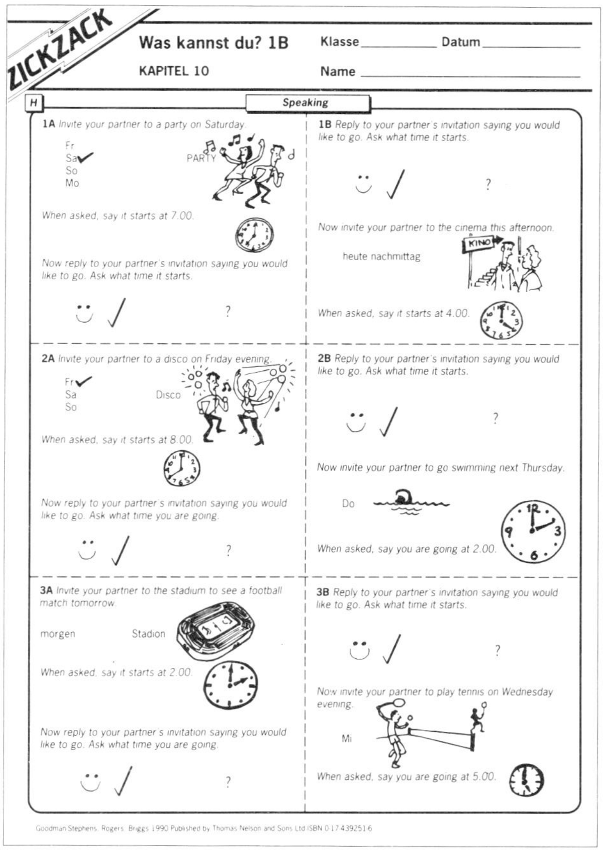
ZICKZACK

Was kannst du? 1B Klasse ________ Datum ________

KAPITEL 10 Name ________

H **Speaking**

1A *Invite your partner to a party on Saturday.*

Fr
Sa ✓
So
Mo

PARTY

When asked, say it starts at 7.00.

Now reply to your partner's invitation saying you would like to go. Ask what time it starts.

✓ ?

1B *Reply to your partner's invitation saying you would like to go. Ask what time it starts.*

✓ ?

Now invite your partner to the cinema this afternoon.

heute nachmittag

KINO

When asked, say it starts at 4.00.

2A *Invite your partner to a disco on Friday evening.*

Fr ✓
Sa
So

Disco

When asked, say it starts at 8.00.

Now reply to your partner's invitation saying you would like to go. Ask what time you are going.

✓ ?

2B *Reply to your partner's invitation saying you would like to go. Ask what time it starts.*

✓ ?

Now invite your partner to go swimming next Thursday.

Do

When asked, say you are going at 2.00.

3A *Invite your partner to the stadium to see a football match tomorrow.*

morgen Stadion

When asked, say it starts at 2.00.

Now reply to your partner's invitation saying you would like to go. Ask what time you are going.

✓ ?

3B *Reply to your partner's invitation saying you would like to go. Ask what time it starts.*

✓ ?

Now invite your partner to play tennis on Wednesday evening.

Mi

When asked, say you are going at 5.00.

Goodman-Stephens, Rogers, Briggs 1990 Published by Thomas Nelson and Sons Ltd ISBN 0-17-439251-6

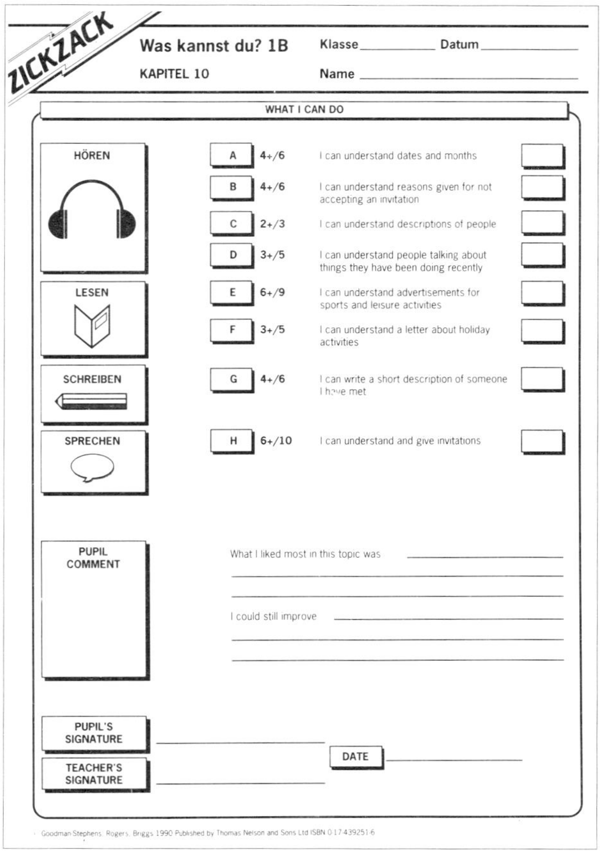
ZICKZACK

Was kannst du? 1B Klasse ________ Datum ________

KAPITEL 10 Name ________

WHAT I CAN DO

HÖREN	A	4+/6	I can understand dates and months	☐
	B	4+/6	I can understand reasons given for not accepting an invitation	☐
	C	2+/3	I can understand descriptions of people	☐
	D	3+/5	I can understand people talking about things they have been doing recently	☐
LESEN	E	6+/9	I can understand advertisements for sports and leisure activities	☐
	F	3+/5	I can understand a letter about holiday activities	☐
SCHREIBEN	G	4+/6	I can write a short description of someone I have met	☐
SPRECHEN	H	6+/10	I can understand and give invitations	☐

PUPIL COMMENT

What I liked most in this topic was ________

I could still improve ________

PUPIL'S SIGNATURE ________

TEACHER'S SIGNATURE ________

DATE ________

Goodman-Stephens, Rogers, Briggs 1990 Published by Thomas Nelson and Sons Ltd ISBN 0-17-439251-6

Kapitel 11

HÖREN

A Understanding illnesses

Tests comprehension of illnesses.

Mir ist schlecht

Beispiel:
– Du, Heike, ich war gestern in dem neuen Restaurant ... und habe Fisch gegessen. Jetzt hab' ich aber Magenschmerzen. Es tut wirklich weh.
– Das tut mir leid. Warst du schon beim Arzt?
– Nein, noch nicht.

1 – Hallo Dieter! Wie geht's?
– Nicht gut.
– Was fehlt dir?
– Ich habe Ohrenschmerzen.
– Schon lange?
– Ja, schon seit zwei Tagen.
2 – Felix, hast du Hustenbonbons?
– Ja, wieso denn?
– Ich hab' Halsschmerzen. Gibst du mir zwei oder drei für die nächste Stunde. In der großen Pause kaufe ich mir welche.
– OK. Hier. Nimm die Tüte.
3 – Du siehst aber schlecht aus, Dorit. Was fehlt dir?
– Mir geht's gar nicht gut. Ich habe fürchterliche Zahnschmerzen. Ich bin auf dem Weg zum Zahnarzt.
– Das tut mir leid. Gute Besserung!
4 – Hast du Lust, Federball zu spielen? Ich geh' heute nachmittag zum Sportzentrum.
– Es tut mir leid. Ich kann im Moment nicht spielen. Mein Arm tut weh.
– Naja, vielleicht ein anderes Mal.
– Ja, gut.

Solution:
1D **2**E **3**C **4**B
Total: **4**

B Understanding sports injuries

Tests comprehension of sports injuries.

Sportskanonen

Beispiel:
– Gestern abend hab' ich Tischtennis mit Inge gespielt. Ich bin aber leider gefallen und hab' mir den Finger gebrochen.
– Tut's weh?
– Ja, und wie!

1 – Wie war's beim Basketballspiel, Dirk? Habt ihr gewonnen?
– Ja, aber ich hab' jetzt Rückenschmerzen.
– Warst du nicht trainiert?
– Nein, ich hatte keine gute Kondition.
– Was machst du jetzt?
– Ich muß ein paar Tage im Bett liegen.
2 – Was ist mit dir passiert, Kurt? Tut's weh?
– Ja. Ich hab' mir den Arm an zwei Stellen gebrochen.
– Was! Wie hast du denn das gemacht?
– Beim Skilaufen bin ich gestürzt.
– Tut mir leid. Gute Besserung.
3 – Hast du dich beim Fußball verletzt?
– Nein, beim Rugby.
– Und ist das Fußgelenk gebrochen?
– Nein, nur verstaucht. In zwei Wochen kann ich wieder spielen.
– Toll!
4 – Mensch, meine Füße tun so weh!
– Was? Deine Füße .. wieso?
– Weißt du nicht? Am Wochenende hab' ich einen halben Marathon gemacht ... über zwanzig Kilometer bin ich gelaufen!
– Bist du doof oder was?
– Ich glaub' schon.

Solution:
1 4A **2** 6B **3** 1F **4** 5C
Total: **8**

C Understanding conversations at the chemist's

Tests comprehension of language at the chemist's.

In der Apotheke

Beispiel:
– Guten Morgen.
– Guten Morgen.
– Ich hätte gern etwas gegen Kopfschmerzen.
– Gegen Kopfschmerzen? Diese Tabletten hier sind sehr gut.
– Was kosten sie?
– Fünf Mark.

1 – Bitte schön.
– Ich brauche etwas gegen Seekrankheit.
– Ich hab' diese Tabletten hier. Die sollen gut sein.
– Wann muß ich die nehmen?
– Zwei Stunden vor der Fahrt.
– OK, danke.
2 – Haben Sie etwas gegen Erkältung?
– Ist das für Sie oder für Ihren Sohn?
– Für mich.
– Haben Sie Fieber?
– Nein.
– Am besten nehmen Sie diese Kapseln. Drei Kapseln pro Tag vor den Mahlzeiten.
– Danke.
3 – Guten Tag. Können Sie mir helfen?
– Ja ...
– Seit drei Tagen hab' ich Heuschnupfen. Haben Sie was dagegen?
– Wollen Sie Tabletten?
– Ja.
– Diese Tabletten sind gut.
– Danke. Sind sie stark?
– Ja, ziemlich.
4 – Guten Tag. Mein Kind hat starke Ohrenschmerzen. Haben Sie etwas dagegen?
– Ihr Kind, sagen Sie?
– Ja, meine Tochter.
– Ja, Sie sollten am besten zu einem Arzt gehen.
– Meinen Sie?
– Ja.

Solution:
1B **2**C **3**A **4**E
Total: **4**

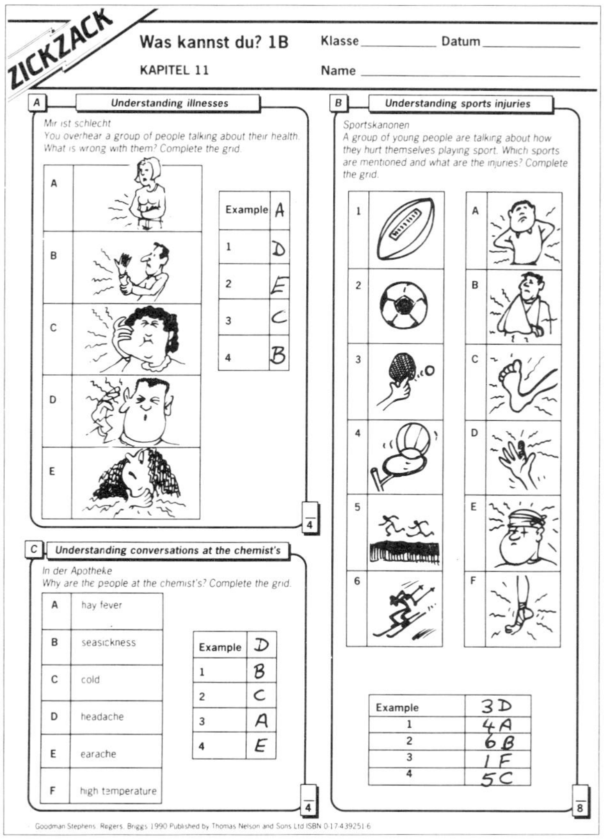

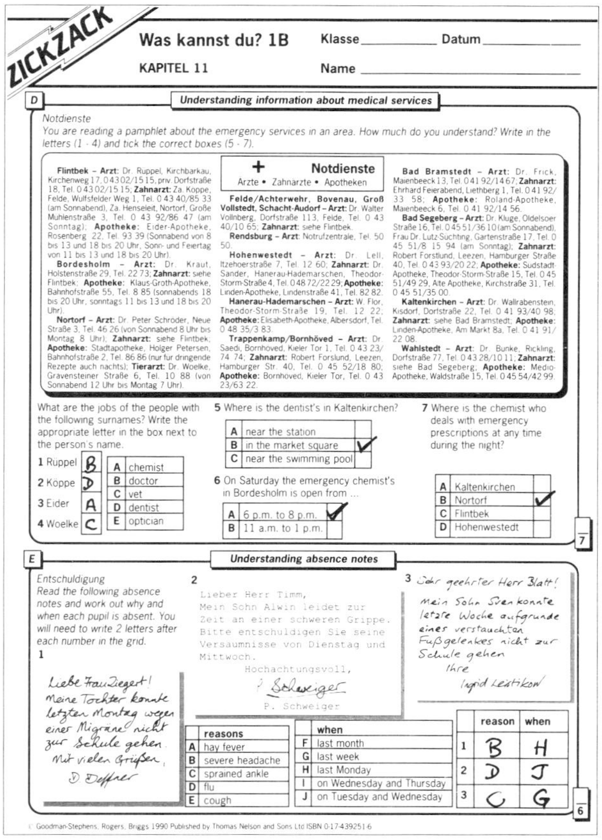

LESEN

D Understanding information about medical services

Tests comprehension of information about medical services.

Solution:
1B **2**D **3**A **4**C **5**B **6**A **7**B
Total: **7**

E Understanding absence notes

Tests comprehension of absence notes.

Solution:
1 BH **2** DJ **3** CG
Total: **6**

F Understanding advertisements for medicines

Tests comprehension of adverts for medicines.

Solution:
1B **2**C **3**B **4**B **5**C
Total: **5**

SCHREIBEN

G Writing

Tests ability to write about allergies and tastes in food and drink.

Marking scheme:
any 6 details from:
Ich esse gern / (*items of food*). / Ich bin allergisch / gegen Käse. / Ich darf nicht (keine)/ Milch / trinken.
Total: **6** (maximum)

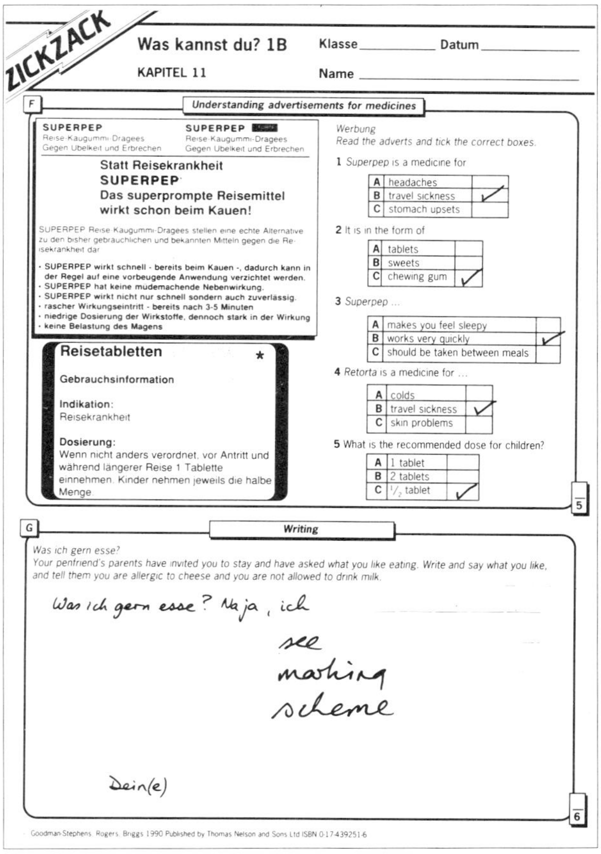

SPRECHEN

H Speaking

Tests ability to make appointments at a doctor's.
Three different sets of pairwork materials. Two activities per pupil in pairwork.
Pupils should be given one of the roles and should then work either with a partner or with the teacher (see Introduction).

Marking scheme:
1 mark per item up to a maximum of 10

1A Guten Tag (Morgen/Abend). / Ich heiße ... (Mein Name ist ...) / Hat Herr/Frau Doktor (am) Montag / (noch) einen Termin frei? / Um wieviel Uhr? / (Danke.) Auf Wiedersehen. / Guten Tag (Morgen/Abend). / Ja, Herr/Frau Doktor hat (am) Mittwoch / einen Termin frei. / Um zehn Uhr. / Auf Wiedersehen.
Total: **10** (maximum)

1B Guten Tag (Morgen/Abend). / Ja, Herr/Frau Doktor hat (am) Montag / einen Termin frei. / Um neun Uhr. / Auf Wiedersehen. / Guten Tag (Morgen/Abend). / Ich heiße ... (Mein Name ist ...) / Hat Herr/Frau Doktor (am) Mittwoch / (noch) einen Termin frei? / Um wieviel Uhr? / (Danke.) Auf Wiedersehen.
Total: **10** (maximum)

2A Guten Tag (Morgen/Abend). / Ich heiße ... (Mein Name ist ...) / Hat Herr/Frau Doktor (am) Freitag / (noch) einen Termin frei? / Um wieviel Uhr? / (Danke.) Auf Wiedersehen. / Guten Tag (Morgen/Abend). / Ja, Herr/Frau Doktor hat (am) Freitag / einen Termin frei. / Um zwanzig vor zehn. / Auf Wiedersehen.
Total: **10** (maximum)

2B Guten Tag (Morgen/Abend). / Ja, Herr/Frau Doktor hat (am) Freitag / einen Termin frei. / Um halb zehn (neun Uhr dreißig). / Auf Wiedersehen. /
Guten Tag (Morgen/Abend). / Ich heiße ... (Mein Name ist ...) / Hat Herr/Frau Doktor (am) Donnerstag / (noch) einen Termin frei? / Um wieviel Uhr? / (Danke.) Auf Wiedersehen.
Total: **10** (maximum)

3A Guten Tag (Morgen/Abend). / Ich heiße ... (Mein Name ist ...) / Hat Herr/Frau Doktor (am) Mittwoch / (noch) einen Termin frei? / Um wieviel Uhr? / (Danke.) Auf Wiedersehen. / Guten Tag (Morgen/Abend). / Ja, Herr/Frau Doktor hat (am) Dienstag / einen Termin frei. / Um halb elf (zehn Uhr dreißig). / Auf Wiedersehen.
Total: **10** (maximum)

3B Guten Tag (Morgen/Abend). / Ja, Herr/Frau Doktor hat (am) Mittwoch / einen Termin frei. / Um zwei Uhr. / Auf Wiedersehen. / Guten Tag (Morgen/Abend). / Ich heiße ... (Mein Name ist ...) / Hat Herr/Frau Doktor (am) Dienstag / (noch) einen Termin frei? / Um wieviel Uhr? / (Danke.) Auf Wiedersehen.
Total: **10** (maximum)

ZICKZACK
Was kannst du? 1B Klasse ______ Datum ______
KAPITEL 11 Name ______

H **Speaking**

1A *Make an appointment at the doctor's. Greet the receptionist then give your name and ask if there is an appointment on Monday. Ask at what time and say goodbye.*
Guten ...
Name
Mo ✓
Di Termin? ?
Mi
Auf ...
Now play the part of the receptionist. Greet the patient. When asked, say there is an appointment on Wednesday. Say it is at 10.00 and say goodbye.
– Guten ......
– Ja, Herr/Frau Doktor hat ...... (Mi)
– Um ......
– Auf ......

1B *Play the part of the receptionist at the doctor's. Greet the patient. When asked, say there is an appointment on Monday. Say it is at 9.00 and say goodbye.*
– Guten ......
– Ja, Herr/Frau Doktor hat ...... (Mo)
– Um ......
– Auf ......
Now play the part of a patient. Greet the receptionist then give your name and ask if there is an appointment on Wednesday. Ask at what time and say goodbye.
Guten ...
Name
Di
Mi ✓ Termin? ?
Do
Auf ...

2A *Make an appointment at the doctor's. Greet the receptionist then give your name and ask if there is an appointment on Friday. Ask at what time and say goodbye.*
Guten ...
Name
Do
Fr ✓ Termin? ?
Sa
Auf ...
Now play the part of the receptionist. Greet the patient. When asked, say there is an appointment on Thursday. Say it is at 9.40 and say goodbye.
– Guten ......
– Ja, Herr/Frau Doktor hat ...... (Do)
– Um ......
– Auf ......

2B *Play the part of the receptionist at the doctor's. Greet the patient. When asked, say there is an appointment on Friday. Say it is at 9.30 and say goodbye.*
– Guten ......
– Ja, Herr/Frau Doktor hat...... (Fr)
– Um ......
– Auf ......
Now play the part of a patient. Greet the receptionist then give your name and ask if there is an appointment on Thursday. Ask at what time and say goodbye.
Guten ...
Name
Mi
Do ✓ Termin? ?
Fr
Auf ...

3A *Make an appointment at the doctor's. Greet the receptionist then give your name and ask if there is an appointment on Wednesday. Ask at what time and say goodbye.*
Guten ...
Name
Mo
Di Termin? ?
Mi ✓
Auf ...
Now play the part of the receptionist. Greet the patient. When asked, say there is an appointment on Tuesday. Say it is at 10.30 and say goodbye.
– Guten ......
– Ja, Herr/Frau Doktor hat ...... (Di)
– Um ......
– Auf ......

3B *Play the part of the receptionist at the doctor's. Greet the patient. When asked, say there is an appointment on Wednesday. Say it is at 2.00 and say goodbye.*
– Guten ......
– Ja, Herr/Frau Doktor hat ...... (Mi)
– Um ......
– Auf ......
Now play the part of a patient. Greet the receptionist then give your name and ask if there is an appointment on Tuesday. Ask at what time and say goodbye.
Guten ...
Name
Mo
Di ✓ Termin? ?
Mi
Auf ...

© Goodman-Stephens, Rogers, Briggs 1990 Published by Thomas Nelson and Sons Ltd ISBN 0-17-439251-6

ZICKZACK
Was kannst du? 1B Klasse ______ Datum ______
KAPITEL 11 Name ______

WHAT I CAN DO

HÖREN	A	3+/4	I can understand illnesses	☐
	B	6+/8	I can understand sports injuries	☐
	C	3+/4	I can understand conversations at the chemist's	☐
LESEN	D	5+/7	I can understand information about medical services	☐
	E	4+/6	I can understand absence notes	☐
	F	3+/5	I can understand advertisements for medicines	☐
SCHREIBEN	G	4+/6	I can write about food and drink I like and allergies	☐
SPRECHEN	H	6+/10	I can book an appointment at the doctor's	☐

PUPIL COMMENT
What I liked most in this topic was ______
I could still improve ______

PUPIL'S SIGNATURE ______
TEACHER'S SIGNATURE ______ DATE ______

Kapitel 12

HÖREN

A Understanding simple details about holiday plans

Tests comprehension of holiday plans, including countries to be visited, length of stay and people accompanying.

Ferienpläne

Beispiel:
Reporter: – Wo fährst du hin?
– Nach Spanien mit meinen Eltern.
– Ja, und für wie lange?
– Eine Woche.

1 – Ich fahre nach Schottland.
Reporter: – Fährst du alleine?
– Nee, mit meiner Freundin. Wir bleiben vierzehn Tage da – in einem Hotel im Gebirge.
2 – Tja, ich fahre nach England und wohne zwei Wochen bei einer Familie in Liverpool.
Reporter: – Fährst du mit Freunden oder ...
– Nein, alleine. Ich fahre zu meinem Brieffreund.
3 – Wir fahren diesmal nach Frankreich.
Reporter: – Fährst du mit deinen Eltern dorthin?
– Nein, mit einer Jugendgruppe. Wir übernachten in Jugendherbergen.
Reporter: – Und wie lange bleibt ihr in Frankreich?
– Drei Wochen.

Solution:

	Destination	with ...	for ...
1	Scotland	(girl)friend	14 days
2	England (Liverpool)	alone/no-one	2 weeks
3	France	youth group	3 weeks

Total: **9**

B Understanding comments about holidays

Tests comprehension of people's comments on the weather and their holiday accommodation.

Auf Urlaub

Beispiel:
– Ja, wir waren in Rom. Es war ein fantastischer Urlaub. Das Wetter war wunderschön, und unser Hotel war sehr bequem.

1 – Der Urlaub war ganz langweilig. Das Wetter war furchtbar – es hat jeden Tag geregnet – und der Campingplatz war auch nicht sehr schön.
2 – Es war ziemlich kalt ... wir waren nämlich in Nordirland, aber die Leute waren nett, und die Jugendherbergen waren toll.
3 – Ich war in Spanien an der Küste. Es war so heiß! Wir hatten jeden Tag Sonne. Das Hotel war aber eine Katastrophe, und das Essen hat mir überhaupt nicht geschmeckt!

Solution:

	Weather	Accommodation
1	awful (rain every day)	not very nice
2	(quite) cold	great
3	hot (sunny)	disaster

Total: **6**

C Understanding holiday activities

Tests comprehension of holiday/leisure activities.

Mein idealer Urlaub

Beispiel:
– Was ich gern mache? Naja, ich gehe gern schwimmen ... ich liege gern in der Sonne, und abends gehe ich gern in die Disco.

1 – Ich verbringe nicht gern den ganzen Tag am Strand. Ich bin ziemlich sportlich, und ich mache gerne Wanderungen und, ja, wie gesagt, ich treibe gerne Sport ... zum Beispiel Tennis. Ich besuche auch gern Sehenswürdigkeiten: Museen, Schlösser und so weiter.
2 – Es gefällt mir am Strand ... ich verbringe den ganzen Tag da, und mache zum Beispiel gern Picknicks. Abends reite ich gern am Strand ... abends ist es dann meistens leer.

Solution:
1K,H,E **2**D,J
Total: **5**

ZICKZACK
Was kannst du? 1B
KAPITEL 12
Klasse ______ Datum ______
Name ______

A Understanding simple details about holiday plans

Ferienpläne
During your holiday visit to Germany you listen to a group of people being interviewed by a travel company representative about their holiday plans. Complete the grid.

	Destination	with ...	for ...
Example	Spain	parents	1 week
1	Scotland	(girl)friend	14 days
2	Liverpool England	alone	2 wks.
3	France	youth group	3 wks.

9

B Understanding comments about holidays

Auf Urlaub
Listen to some people talking about the holidays they have just been on and complete the grid.

	Weather	Accommodation
Example	wonderful	very comfortable
1	terrible	not very nice
2	quite cold	great
3	very hot	a disaster

6

C Understanding holiday activities

Mein idealer Urlaub
You are watching a TV programme about travel and holidays, in which people talk about their favourite holiday activities. Match the pictures to the activities mentioned and complete the grid.

	Activities		
Example	A	B	C
1	K	H	E
2	D	J	—

5

© Goodman-Stephens, Rogers, Briggs 1990 Published by Thomas Nelson and Sons Ltd ISBN 0-17-439251-6

LESEN

D Understanding a travel brochure

Tests comprehension of a travel brochure.

Solution:
1A **2**B **3**D **4**A **5**A **6**C
Total: **6**

E Understanding campsite material

Tests comprehension of campsite advertising materials.

Solution:
1T **2**T **3**T **4**F **5**T **6**T **7**F **8**T
Total: **8**

SCHREIBEN

F Writing

An open-ended task which tests ability to write a postcard about a holiday.

Marking scheme:
6 details from
Ich bin (wir sind) / in (*place*). / Das Wetter ist (es ist) / heiß (warm/kalt/etc.)/fantastisch (mies etc.).
Ich schwimme (faulenze/etc.) / jeden Tag (meistens vormittags). / Abends / gehe ich / in die Disco (ins Kino/etc.)
Total: **6** (maximum)

ZICKZACK

Was kannst du? 1B Klasse ________ Datum ________

KAPITEL 12 Name ________

D — *Understanding a travel brochure*

Schottland-Reise
Read the brochure and tick the appropriate boxes.

SCHOTTLAND-REISE

INKLUSIVPREIS S 11.540,-

inbegriffen sind: Flug nach London und retour, Transfer vom Flughafen Gatwick nach London und zurück, Rundreise nach Schottland wie nebenstehend, 2 Übernachtungen in London, 3 in Edinburgh, 2 in den Highlands, täglich englisches Frühstück, in Schottland 5 Abendessen und 3 Mittagessen, Unterkunft in Zweibettzimmern mit Bad/Wc.

REISEPROGRAMM

Mittwoch: Flug ab Wien – Übernachtung im Onslow Court Hotel, South Kensington.
Donnerstag: Abfahrt von London mit Autobus der "Scottish Omnibuses" über Penrith nach Edinburgh – Übernachtung.
Freitag: Freier Tag in Edinburgh mit Übernachtung. Eine Stadtrundfahrt mit Führung kann örtlich um ca. 6 Pfund gebucht werden.
Samstag: Fahrt mit (englischsprachiger) Führung in die Berge und zu den Seen des schottischen Hochlands – Falkirk, Stirling, Callander, Lochearnhead, Killin (Mittagessen), Tyndrum, Bridge of Orchy, Moor of Rannoch, Glen Coe, Fort William, Fort Augustus, Übernachtung im Drumnadrochit Hotel am Loch Ness.
Sonntag: Fahrt zu den Fjorden der Westküste – Glen Convinth, Beauly, Falls of Rogie (Wasserfälle), Garvie, Kinlochewe, Loch Maree, Gairloch, Inverewe Gardens (Mittagessen), Loch Ewe, Albea, Gruinard Bay, Dundonnell, Aultguish, Beauly, Inverness, Übernachtung im Drumnadrochit Hotel.
Montag: Fahrt durch die Berge und Städte Mittelschottlands, Inverness, Culloden Moor, Kingussie, Newtonmore, Dalwhinnie (Mittagessen), Pass of Killiecrankie, Pitlochry, Dunkeld, Amulree, Crieff, Gleneagles, Glen Devon, Dunfermline, Forth Road Bridge, Übernachtung in Edinburgh.
Dienstag: Rückfahrt per Bus nach London mit Übernachtung im Onslow Court Hotel.
Mittwoch: Heimflug nach Wien.

Anglo-Austrian Society

1 This is an advertisement for a trip from:
A Austria to Scotland ✓
B Germany to Scotland
C Switzerland to Scotland

2 They will stay overnight in:
A 5 places
B 3 places ✓
C 2 places

3 The accommodation will consist of:
A single rooms with a bath
B double rooms with a shower
C family rooms with a bath
D double rooms with a bath ✓

4 Travel from London to Scotland is by:
A bus ✓
B train
C plane

5 The tour of the Scottish Highlands takes place on:
A Saturday ✓
B Sunday
C Monday

6 The tour of Central Scotland takes place on:
A Saturday
B Sunday
C Monday ✓

6

Goodman-Stephens, Rogers, Briggs 1990 Published by Thomas Nelson and Sons Ltd ISBN 0-17-439251-6

ZICKZACK

Was kannst du? 1B Klasse ________ Datum ________

KAPITEL 12 Name ________

E — *Understanding campsite material*

Grüß Gott **im Kur-Camping Arterhof**

Sommer- und Winter-Camping

Unser Komfort-Campingplatz in ruhiger, reizvoller und landschaftlich schöner Umgebung lädt Sie zum KUR-BADE-Aufenthalt ein. Der naheliegende Wald führt zu erholsamen Wander- und Spaziergängen. Der CAMPINGPLATZ (2 ha) verfügt über 50 Stellplätze – Dauerstellplätze mit ca. 100 m² je Standplatz. Der Platz ist eben, befestigt und trocken. Moderne sanitäre Einrichtungen stehen unseren Gästen zur Verfügung – 12 Waschbecken – 10 Duschkabinen – 12 Toiletten – Geschirrspülraum – Wäscheraum mit Waschmaschine – Trockner und chem. WC. Entfliehen Sie der Hektik des Alltags und erholen Sie sich auf unserem Platz, der Ihnen die Ruhe und Entspannung in ländlicher Idylle bietet.

Wir freuen uns auf Ihren Besuch und wünschen Ihnen einen angenehmen Aufenthalt. Familie Sigl

Campingplatz ARTERHOF
Fam. Josef und Mina Sigl
Lengham - Hauptstraße 3
D-8345 BIRNBACH/Rottal
Telefon 0 85 63/8 08

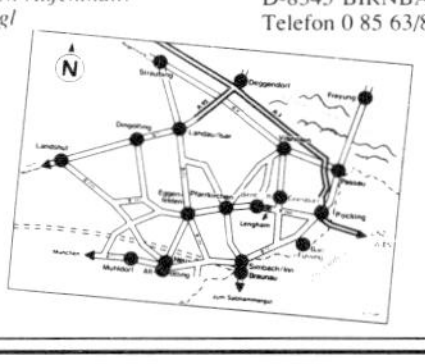

1 T
2 T
3 T
4 F
5 T
6 T
7 F
8 T

8

F — *Writing*

Hallo Jutta!
You are writing a postcard whilst on holiday to your German penfriend. Say where you are, what the weather is like and what you are doing during your holiday.

Hallo Jutta!

see marking scheme

Jutta Forster
Feldstraße 45
4600 Dortmund

6

Goodman-Stephens, Rogers, Briggs 1990 Published by Thomas Nelson and Sons Ltd ISBN 0-17-439251-6

SPRECHEN

G Speaking

Tests ability to book in at a campsite.
Three different sets of pairwork materials. Two activities per pupil in pairwork.
Pupils should be given one of the roles and should then work either with a partner or with the teacher (see Introduction).

Marking scheme:
2 marks per item up to a maximum of 10

1A Haben Sie (Ist hier) noch Platz frei?
Drei Nächte.
Vier Personen – zwei Erwachsene und zwei Kinder.
Acht und zehn (Jahre alt).
Nein (, wir haben kein Zelt). Wir haben einen Wagen (ein Auto) und einen Wohnwagen.
(Das macht) fünfzig Mark.
Total: **10** (maximum)

1B (Das macht) fünfunddreißig Mark.
Haben Sie (Ist hier) noch Platz frei?
Zwei Nächte.
Fünf Personen – zwei Erwachsene und drei Kinder.
Vier, sechs und neun (Jahre alt).
Nein (, wir haben keinen Wohnwagen). Wir haben einen Wagen (ein Auto) und ein Zelt.
Total: **10** (maximum)

2A Haben Sie (Ist hier) noch Platz frei?
Vier Nächte.
Zwei Personen – ein(e) Erwachsene(r) und ein Kind.
Zwölf (Jahre alt).
Nein (, wir haben keinen Wohnwagen). Wir haben einen Wagen (ein Auto) und ein Zelt.
(Das macht) vierzig Mark.
Total: **10** (maximum)

2B (Das macht) fünfundvierzig Mark.
Haben Sie (Ist hier) noch Platz frei?
Eine Nacht.
Fünf Personen – drei Erwachsene und zwei Kinder.
Drei und fünf (Jahre alt).
Nein (, wir haben kein Zelt). Wir haben einen Wagen (ein Auto) und einen Wohnwagen.
Total: **10** (maximum)

3A Haben Sie (Ist hier) noch Platz frei?
Zwei Nächte.
Vier Personen – ein(e) Erwachsene(r) und zwei Kinder.
Elf und dreizehn (Jahre alt).
Nein (, wir haben keinen Wohnwagen). Wir haben einen Wagen (ein Auto) und ein Zelt.
(Das macht) fünfzig Mark.
Total: **10** (maximum)

3B (Das macht) fünfunddreißig Mark.
Haben Sie (Ist hier) noch Platz frei?
Zwei Nächte.
Vier Personen – zwei Erwachsene und zwei Kinder.
Fünf und sieben (Jahre alt).
Nein (, wir haben kein Zelt). Wir haben einen Wagen (ein Auto) und einen Wohnwagen.
Total: **10** (maximum)

ZICKZACK
Was kannst du? 1B Klasse ________ Datum ________
KAPITEL 12 Name ________

G **Speaking**

1A *Book in at a campsite. Ask if there's any room, then answer the warden's questions: say you are staying 3 nights, there are 2 adults and 2 children (aged 8 and 10) and you have a car and caravan.*
Platz? 3x
8+10
Now play the part of the warden. Answer the customer's question, ask the following questions and finally give the cost.
— Ja ... wie lange wollen Sie bleiben?
— Wieviel Personen sind Sie?
— Wie alt sind die Kinder?
— Haben Sie einen Wohnwagen?
— Das macht DM 50,-.

1B *Play the part of a campsite warden. Answer the customer's question, then ask the following questions and finally give the cost.*
— Ja ... wie lange wollen Sie bleiben?
— Wieviel Personen sind Sie?
— Wie alt sind die Kinder?
— Haben Sie ein Zelt?
— Das macht DM 35,-.
Now you play the part of a customer booking in. Ask if there's any room, then answer the warden's questions: say you are staying 2 nights, there are 2 adults and 3 children (aged 4, 6 and 9) and you have a car and tent.
Platz? 2 x
4 + 6 + 9

2A *Book in at a campsite. Ask if there's any room, then answer the warden's questions: say you are staying 4 nights, there are 1 adult and 1 child (aged 12) and you have a car and tent.*
Platz? 4 x
12
Now play the part of the warden. Answer the customer's question, ask the following questions and finally give the cost.
— Ja ... wie lange wollen Sie bleiben?
— Wieviel Personen sind Sie?
— Wie alt sind die Kinder?
— Haben Sie ein Zelt?
— Das macht DM 40,-.

2B *Play the part of a campsite warden. Answer the customer's question, then ask the following questions and finally give the cost.*
— Ja ... wie lange wollen Sie bleiben?
— Wieviel Personen sind Sie?
— Wie alt ist das Kind?
— Haben Sie einen Wohnwagen?
— Das macht DM 45,-.
Now you play the part of a customer booking in. Ask if there's any room, then answer the warden's questions: say you are staying 1 night, there are 3 adults and 2 children (aged 3 and 5) and you have a car and caravan.
Platz? 1 x
3 + 5

3A *Book in at a campsite. Ask if there's any room, then answer the warden's questions: say you are staying 2 nights, there are 1 adult and 2 children (aged 11 and 13) and you have a car and tent.*
Platz? 2 x
11 + 13
Now play the part of the warden. Answer the customer's question, ask the following questions and finally give the cost.
— Ja ... wie lange wollen Sie bleiben?
— Wieviel Personen sind Sie?
— Wie alt sind die Kinder?
— Haben Sie ein Zelt?
— Das macht DM 100,-.

3B *Play the part of a campsite warden. Answer the customer's question, then ask the following questions and finally give the cost.*
— Ja ... wie lange wollen Sie bleiben?
— Wieviel Personen sind Sie?
— Wie alt sind die Kinder?
— Haben Sie einen Wohnwagen?
— Das macht DM 25,-.
Now you play the part of a customer booking in. Ask if there's any room, then answer the warden's questions: say you are staying 5 nights, there are 2 adults and 2 children (aged 5 and 7) and you have a car and caravan.
Platz? 5 x
5 + 7

Goodman Stephens, Rogers, Briggs 1990 Published by Thomas Nelson and Sons Ltd ISBN 0-17-439251-6

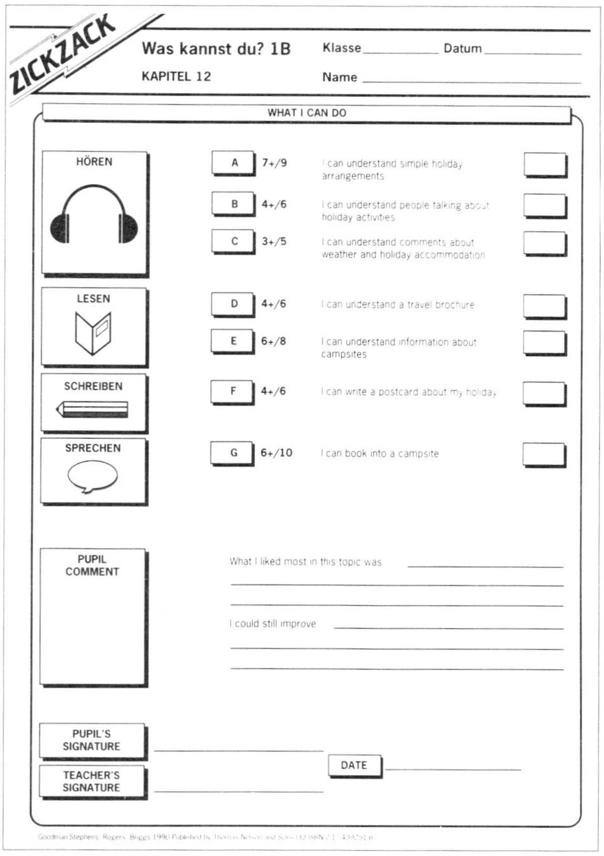

ZICKZACK
Was kannst du? 1B Klasse ________ Datum ________
KAPITEL 12 Name ________

WHAT I CAN DO

HÖREN	A	7+/9	I can understand simple holiday arrangements	
	B	4+/6	I can understand people talking about holiday activities	
	C	3+/5	I can understand comments about weather and holiday accommodation	
LESEN	D	4+/6	I can understand a travel brochure	
	E	6+/8	I can understand information about campsites	
SCHREIBEN	F	4+/6	I can write a postcard about my holiday	
SPRECHEN	G	6+/10	I can book into a campsite	

PUPIL COMMENT
What I liked most in this topic was ________
I could still improve ________

PUPIL'S SIGNATURE ________
TEACHER'S SIGNATURE ________
DATE ________

Goodman Stephens, Rogers, Briggs 1990 Published by Thomas Nelson and Sons Ltd ISBN 0-17-439251-6

Attainment Test Kapitel 7-12

HÖREN

A Understanding general conversations

Tests gist comprehension of short dialogues based on situations in chapters 7-12.

Wohnst du in Hamburg?

1 – Wohnst du in Hamburg?
– Nein, in Köln.
– Was gibt es da zu sehen?
– Den Dom und viele Museen, die Universität und ein schönes Einkaufszentrum.
2 – Entschuldigung, ich suche das Freibad.
– Moment mal ... ja, das ist hinter der Kirche. Also, hier gleich links um die Ecke.
– Danke schön.
3 – Guten Tag.
– Guten Tag. Kann ich Ihnen helfen?
– Ja. Haben Sie einen Stadtplan und ein Hotelverzeichnis?
– Ja, bitte schön.
– Danke.
4 – Entschuldigung, können Sie mir sagen, wo die nächste U-Bahnstation ist?
– Die nächste U-Bahnstation?
– Ja, ist das weit von hier?
– Nein, nicht weit. 200 bis 300 Meter. Sie gehen hier geradeaus, dann die zweite Straße links rein. Die U-Bahn ist auf der rechten Seite.
5 – Bitte schön?
– 200 Gramm Schinken und 300 Gramm Leberwurst.
– So, bitte schön. Sonst noch etwas?
– Danke, das ist alles.
6 – Hallo Sven. Kommst du heute zum Sportplatz?
– Ja, natürlich. Wie kommst du dahin? Bringt dich deine Mutter mit dem Auto, oder ... ?
– Nein, leider nicht. Ich gehe zu Fuß. Und du?
– Mit dem Mofa.
7 – Wie findest du Jürgen?
– Wer ist das?
– Der Große mit der Lederjacke.
– Ach der ... ich finde ihn sehr nett. Seinen Bruder kann ich aber nicht leiden.
8 – Hallo Ute, wie geht's?
– Och, es geht.
– Ich meinte ... ich gehe heute abend ins Jugendzentrum. Kommst du mit?
– Ja, gerne. Um wieviel Uhr?
– So gegen halb sieben. Ich hol' dich ab.
– Toll!
9 – Mutti, muß ich heute in die Schule?
– Was fehlt dir denn?
– Ich habe furchtbare Kopfschmerzen.
– Moment mal ... oh, du Arme, du hast Fieber, ja. Geh mal wieder ins Bett. Ich rufe sofort den Arzt an.
10 – In den Sommerferien fahre ich gern an die See. Ich liege ganz gern in der Sonne, und ich gehe gern schwimmen.
– Ich nicht. Ich fahre lieber in die Berge.

Solution:
1E **2**H **3**N **4**C **5**I **6**M **7**G **8**D **9**A **10**L
Total: **10**

ZICKZACK **Was kannst du? 1B** Klasse ______ Datum ______
KAPITEL 7-12 Name ______

A Understanding general conversations

Wohnst du in Hamburg?
You hear a number of people in different situations having short conversations. What are they about? Write the correct letters in the boxes.

A Someone feeling ill
B Buying stamps at a Post Office
C Asking the way to the Underground
D Arranging to go out with someone
E Facilities in a town
F Buying tickets at a railway station
G Opinions people have of others
H Finding the swimming pool
I Buying food
J People saying what they have been doing
K Making an appointment at the dentist's
L Types of holiday people prefer
M Different ways of travelling to the sports ground
N Materials and information in a Tourist Office

1	2	3	4	5	6	7	8	9	10
E	H	N	C	I	M	G	D	A	L

10

B Understanding Post Office language

Auf der Post
You overhear the customer in front of you at the Post Office counter.

POST

1 What does she buy?
20 stamps
2 How much does each one cost?
60 Pfennig
3 What is the total cost?
DM 12,–

3

C Understanding a department store assistant

Im Kaufhaus
The girl in front of you is talking to the assistant.

1 What does she want to buy?
earrings
2 How much do they cost?
DM 17,–
3 How much are the next ones the assistant shows her?
DM 11,–
4 What does the girl say before she buys them?
that she likes them

4

© Goodman-Stephens, Rogers, Briggs 1990 Published by Thomas Nelson and Sons Ltd ISBN 0-17-439251-6

ZICKZACK **Was kannst du? 1B** Klasse ______ Datum ______
KAPITEL 7-12 Name ______

D Understanding language in a chemist's

In der Apotheke
You listen to another customer talking to the chemist.

1 What is the customer suffering from?
hay fever
2 What is recommended?
tablets
3 How much are they?
DM 8,– (a packet)
4 What is the customer offered for DM 13,- ?
capsules
5 What other means of treatment is mentioned?
injection
6 What does the chemist finally recommend?
go to a doctor

6

E Understanding language at the railway station

Auf dem Bahnhof
Listen to the conversation then fill in the gaps in the text.

The customer wants a return ticket to Göttingen. It costs DM 35,-. The next train to Göttingen leaves at 16.15 from platform 5. He will not have to change trains.

5

F Understanding railway announcements

Vorsicht bei der Abfahrt
You hear two announcements. What do they tell you? Tick the appropriate box.

1

A	All change.	
B	We apologise for the delay.	
C	The doors close automatically.	✓

2

A	We apologise for the delay.	
B	All change.	✓
C	The train to Munich is cancelled due to engine failure.	

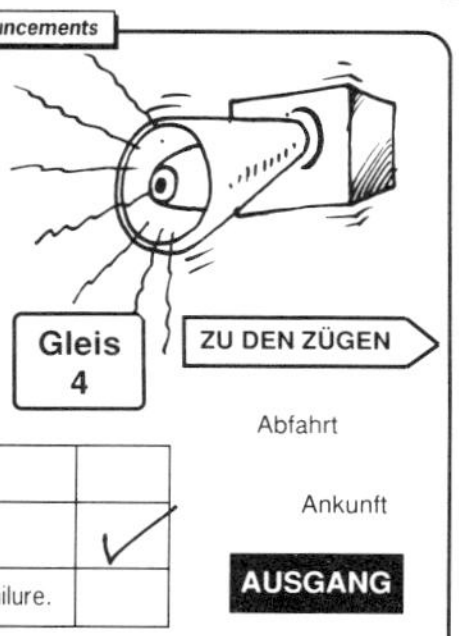

2

© Goodman-Stephens, Rogers, Briggs 1990 Published by Thomas Nelson and Sons Ltd ISBN 0-17-439251-6

B Understanding Post Office language

Tests detailed comprehension of Post Office language.

Auf der Post

– Guten Tag.
– Guten Tag. Zwanzig Briefmarken zu sechzig.
– Zwanzig?
– Ja.
– Bitte schön. Das macht zwölf Mark.
– Danke.

Solution:
1 20 stamps **2** 60 Pfennig **3** DM 12,-
Total: **3**

C Understanding a department store assistant

Tests detailed comprehension of shopping in a department store.

Im Kaufhaus

– Ja, guten Tag. Darf ich Ihnen helfen?
– Ja, ich hätte gern diese Ohrringe. Was kosten sie?
– Diese hier?
– Ja.
– DM 17,-.
– Oh, das ist mir ein bißchen zu teuer.
– Wir haben hier eine große Auswahl. Diese Ohrringe hier zum Beispiel kosten nur DM 11,-. Das ist ganz preiswert.
– Ja, die gefallen mir. Die nehme ich.

Solution:
1 earrings **2** DM 17,-
3 DM 11,- **4** (she) likes them
Total: **4**

D Understanding language in a chemist's

Tests detailed comprehension of language at the chemist's.

In der Apotheke

– Guten Morgen.
– Guten Morgen. Kann ich Ihnen behilflich sein?
– Ich hätte gern etwas gegen Heuschnupfen.
– Dann empfehle ich diese Tabletten hier.
– Was kostet die Packung?
– DM 8,- ... wir haben auch diese Kapseln hier. Sie kosten DM 13,-.
– Tja, ich weiß nicht ...
– Sonst müssen Sie zum Arzt ... für eine Spritze.
– Was würden Sie empfehlen?
– Ich glaube, am besten sollten Sie zu einem Arzt gehen.
– Vielen Dank für die Hilfe.

Solution:
1 hay fever **4** capsules
2 tablets **5** injection
3 DM 8,- (packet) **6** go to doctor's (injection)
Total: **6**

E Understanding language at the railway station

Tests detailed comprehension of buying tickets.

Auf dem Bahnhof

– Bitte schön?
– Einmal nach Göttingen.
– Einfach oder hin und zurück?
– Einfach.
– Bitte schön. DM 35,-.
– Wann fährt der nächste Zug?
– Der nächste Zug fährt planmäßig um 16.15 Uhr.
– Von welchem Gleis?
– Gleis fünf.
– Muß ich umsteigen?
– Nein.

Solution:
1 single
2 (DM) 35,-
3 16.15 (4.15)
4 platform 5
5 change (trains)
Total: **5**

F Understanding railway announcements

Tests detailed comprehension of railway announcements.

Vorsicht bei der Abfahrt

1 – Am Gleis vier bitte einsteigen. Türen schließen selbsttätig. Vorsicht bei der Abfahrt.
2 – München Hauptbahnhof. München Hauptbahnhof. Bitte alle aussteigen. Die Zugfahrt endet hier. Alle aussteigen, bitte.

Solution:
1C **2**B
Total: **2**

LESEN

G Understanding a shopping list for food and drink

Tests comprehension of food and containers and measures.

Solution:
1E **2**F **3**G **4**I
Total: **4**

H Understanding a holiday postcard

Tests comprehension of a holiday postcard dealing with weather and various activities.

Solution:
1B **2**B **3**A **4**B
Total: **4**

I Understanding a railway timetable

Tests comprehension of a railway timetable.

Solution:
1F **2**F **3**T
Total: **3**

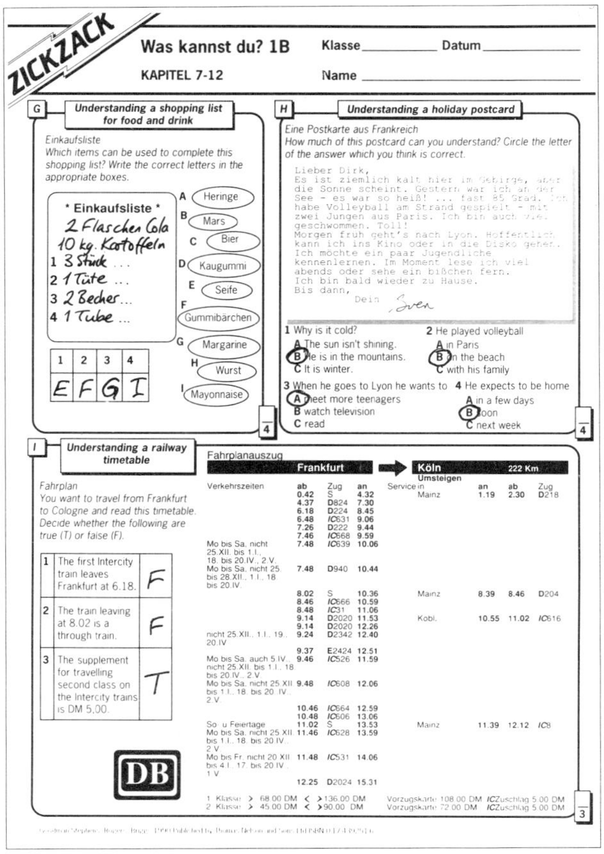

ZICKZACK **Was kannst du? 1B** Klasse ________ Datum ________
KAPITEL 7-12 Name ________

G Understanding a shopping list for food and drink

Einkaufsliste
Which items can be used to complete this shopping list? Write the correct letters in the appropriate boxes.

* Einkaufsliste *
2 Flaschen Cola
10 kg. Kartoffeln
1 3 Stück ...
2 1 Tüte ...
3 2 Becher ...
4 1 Tube ...

A Heringe
B Mars
C Bier
D Kaugummi
E Seife
F Gummibärchen
G Margarine
H Wurst
I Mayonnaise

1	2	3	4
E	F	G	I

4

H Understanding a holiday postcard

Eine Postkarte aus Frankreich
How much of this postcard can you understand? Circle the letter of the answer which you think is correct.

Lieber Dirk,
Es ist ziemlich kalt hier im Gebirge, aber die Sonne scheint. Gestern war ich an der See - es war so heiß! ... fast 85 Grad. Ich habe Volleyball am Strand gespielt - mit zwei Jungen aus Paris. Ich bin auch viel geschwommen. Toll!
Morgen früh geht's nach Lyon. Hoffentlich kann ich ins Kino oder in die Disko gehen. Ich möchte ein paar Jugendliche kennenlernen. Im Moment lese ich viel abends oder sehe ein bißchen fern.
Ich bin bald wieder zu Hause.
Bis dann,
Dein Sven

1 Why is it cold?
A The sun isn't shining.
(B) He is in the mountains.
C It is winter.

2 He played volleyball
A in Paris
(B) on the beach
C with his family

3 When he goes to Lyon he wants to
(A) meet more teenagers
B watch television
C read

4 He expects to be home
A in a few days
(B) soon
C next week

4

I Understanding a railway timetable

Fahrplan
You want to travel from Frankfurt to Cologne and read this timetable. Decide whether the following are true (T) or false (F).

1	The first Intercity train leaves Frankfurt at 6.18.	F
2	The train leaving at 8.02 is a through train.	F
3	The supplement for travelling second class on the Intercity trains is DM 5,00.	T

Fahrplanauszug
Frankfurt → Köln 222 Km

Verkehrszeiten	ab	Zug	an	Service	Umsteigen in	an	ab	Zug
	0.42	S	4.32		Mainz	1.19	2.30	D218
	4.37	D824	7.30					
	6.18	D224	8.45					
	6.48	IC631	9.06					
	7.26	D222	9.44					
	7.46	IC668	9.59					
Mo bis Sa, nicht 25.XII. bis 1.I., 18. bis 20.IV., 2.V.	7.48	IC639	10.06					
Mo bis Sa, nicht 25. bis 28.XII., 1.I., 18 bis 20.IV.	7.48	D940	10.44					
	8.02	S	10.36		Mainz	8.39	8.46	D204
	8.46	IC666	10.59					
	8.48	IC31	11.06					
	9.14	D2020	11.53		Kobl.	10.55	11.02	IC616
	9.14	D2020	12.26					
nicht 25.XII., 1.I., 19., 20.IV	9.24	D2342	12.40					
	9.37	E2424	12.51					
Mo bis Sa. auch 5.IV., nicht 25.XII. bis 1.I., 18. bis 20.IV., 2.V.	9.46	IC526	11.59					
Mo bis Sa. nicht 25.XII. bis 1.I., 18. bis 20. IV., 2.V.	9.48	IC608	12.06					
	10.46	IC664	12.59					
	10.48	IC606	13.06					
So. u Feiertage	11.02	S	13.53		Mainz	11.39	12.12	IC8
Mo bis Sa. nicht 25.XII. bis 1.I., 18. bis 20.IV., 2.V.	11.46	IC628	13.59					
Mo bis Fr. nicht 20.XII. bis 4.I., 17. bis 20.IV., 1.V.	11.48	IC531	14.06					
	12.25	D2024	15.31					

1. Klasse > 68.00 DM < >136.00 DM Vorzugskarte 108.00 DM ICZuschlag 5.00 DM
2. Klasse > 45.00 DM < >90.00 DM Vorzugskarte 72.00 DM ICZuschlag 5.00 DM

DB

3

J Understanding advertisements

Tests comprehension of sports and extra-curricular activities in advertisements.

Solution:
1H **2**A **3**B **4**I
Total: **4**

ZICKZACK **Was kannst du? 1B** Klasse ________ Datum ________
KAPITEL 7-12 Name ________

J Understanding advertisements

Sport und Freizeit
You are looking at the Yellow Pages in Germany in order to find out about sports and other activities. Complete the grid at the foot of the page.

A
SportHütte
Alles für den Sport
Gr. Burstah 36 . Tel. 36 75 76
gleich hinterm Rathaus

B
Bergsportzentrale
Grindelberg 77
200 Hamburg 13
(040) 44 92 83
Bergsport Zentrale
Schlafsäcke . Rucksäcke . Zelte . Outdoor-Kleidung . Bergsport . Bücher . Schuhe Zubehör . Langlauf-Ski . Touren-Ski

C
Fitness-Center TOP FIT
Inh. Meinhard Kleemann
* Fitnesstraining
* Bodybuilding
* Gewichtsregulierung
* Sauna.Sonnenbank
IFBB
Tel. 77 44 40
Lüneburger Tor 8 . 2100 Hamburg 90

H
SPORTING-LIVE
FITNESS-OASE
wo Fitness Spaß macht
Schwimmbad . Whirlpool . Sauna
Solarien . Massage . Kosmetik
Robert-Koch-Str. 26 Hmb. 20 (Eppendorf)
47 20 75/76

D
Tischtennis-Mini-Shop Norderstedt
M. Sillus 15-18 Uhr u.n. Vereinbarung
Langenharmer Weg 55 E 5 26 15 31

I
Colón
Hamburgs größte priv. Sprachenschule
Alle Sprachen . Gruppen und Einzelunterricht
Tages- und Abendklassen
Konversationszirkel . Intensivklassen
Sprachen für Industrie und Wirtschaft
Firmenunterricht . Bildungsurlaub . Ferienkurse
Fortbildung und Umschulung:
zur Sekretärin . zur Fremdsprachensekretärin
zur Fremdsprachenkorrespondentin
Handelsschule fremdsprachlicher Richtung
Kurzschrift und Maschinenschreiben
Deutsch für Ausländer
Fremdsprachenbuchhandlung und Cafeteria im Haus
Colonnaden 47 . 2000 Hamburg 36
Tel:34 58 84 Tel:34 58 50
Tel:34 67 64
Bergstraße 1-9, CCR . 2057 Reinbek
Tel:7 22 73 95

E
Jumbo-Judo 46 48 68
Judo Ju-Jitsu Karate Gymnastik
Fitness Damen + Herren Sonnenbank
Winterhuder Marktplatz 10 Hmb 60

F
Känguruh-Sport 5 27 44 34
und Freizeittreff
für Kinder und Erwachsene
62 Essener-99 100 m U-Ochsenzoll

G
Fitness-Training
Body-Styling
Aero-Gymnastik
Ballett Kindersport
Jazz-Gymnastik
Judo Kick-Boxen
Taekwondo Karate
Ju-Jitsu Yoga
Finn. Sauna
Röm. Dampfbad
Sonnenstudio
Optimale Trainingszeiten
Mo. - Fr. 9-22 Uhr
Sa. u. So. 10-18 Uhr
FREIZEIT . FITNESS . GESUNDHEIT
juka dojo
SPORTCENTER
Fuhlsbüttel
Hummelsb. Landstr. 98
59 83 01
Nienstedten
Langenhegen 9a-d
82 37 48
Rahlstedt
Rahlstedt CENTER
677 50 44
Steilshoop
Gründgensstr. 26
630 11 07

	Find out	advert
1	where you can go swimming	H
2	a shop near the town hall which sells all sorts of sports goods	A
3	a shop which sells camping equipment	B
4	a place where you can improve your German	I

4

© Goodman-Stephens, Rogers, Briggs 1990 Published by Thomas Nelson and Sons Ltd ISBN 0-17-439251-6

K Understanding a programme of events

Tests comprehension of a programme of activities for young people..

Solution:
1 Wednesdays + Sunday (22nd) **2**
2 Thursday - Saturday (Th., Fr., Sat.) **2**
3 Saturday
Total: **5**

L Understanding an advertisement in a newspaper

Tests comprehension of an advertisement for an excursion to an international soccer match, including details of travel, times, accommodation and cost.

Solution:
1T **2**F **3**F **4**F **5**T **6**F **7**F **8**T **9**F **10**F
Total: **10**

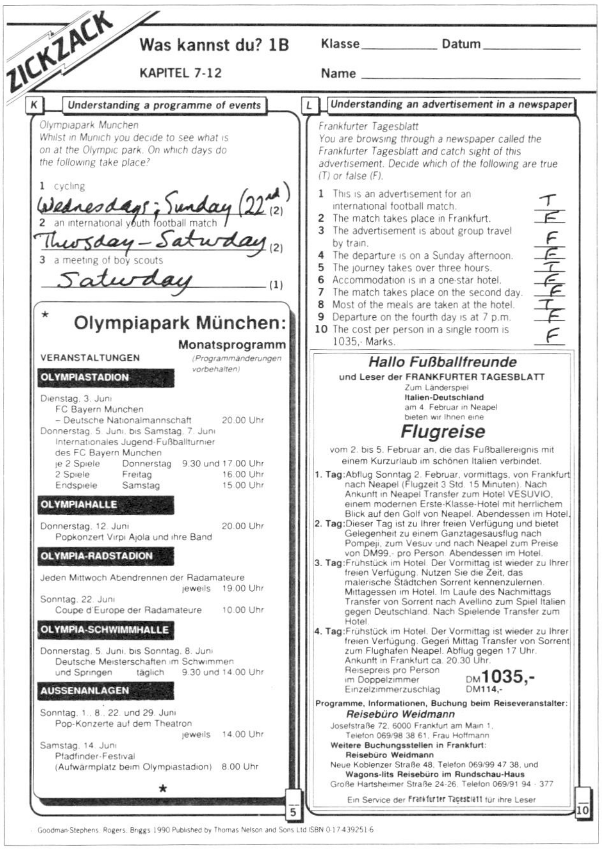

ZICKZACK

Was kannst du? 1B Klasse ____________ Datum ____________

KAPITEL 7-12 Name ____________

K **Understanding a programme of events**

Olympiapark München
Whilst in Munich you decide to see what is on at the Olympic park. On which days do the following take place?

1 cycling
Wednesdays; Sunday (22nd) (2)
2 an international youth football match
Thursday – Saturday (2)
3 a meeting of boy scouts
Saturday (1)

* **Olympiapark München:**
Monatsprogramm
VERANSTALTUNGEN *(Programmänderungen vorbehalten)*

OLYMPIASTADION
Dienstag, 3. Juni
FC Bayern München
– Deutsche Nationalmannschaft 20.00 Uhr
Donnerstag, 5. Juni, bis Samstag, 7. Juni
Internationales Jugend-Fußballturnier des FC Bayern München
je 2 Spiele Donnerstag 9.30 und 17.00 Uhr
2 Spiele Freitag 16.00 Uhr
Endspiele Samstag 15.00 Uhr

OLYMPIAHALLE
Donnerstag, 12. Juni 20.00 Uhr
Popkonzert Virpi Ajola und ihre Band

OLYMPIA-RADSTADION
Jeden Mittwoch Abendrennen der Radamateure jeweils 19.00 Uhr
Sonntag, 22. Juni
Coupe d'Europe der Radamateure 10.00 Uhr

OLYMPIA-SCHWIMMHALLE
Donnerstag, 5. Juni, bis Sonntag, 8. Juni
Deutsche Meisterschaften im Schwimmen und Springen täglich 9.30 und 14.00 Uhr

AUSSENANLAGEN
Sonntag, 1., 8., 22. und 29. Juni
Pop-Konzerte auf dem Theatron jeweils 14.00 Uhr
Samstag, 14. Juni
Pfadfinder-Festival
(Aufwärmplatz beim Olympiastadion) 8.00 Uhr

*

5

L **Understanding an advertisement in a newspaper**

Frankfurter Tagesblatt
You are browsing through a newspaper called the Frankfurter Tagesblatt and catch sight of this advertisement. Decide which of the following are true (T) or false (F).

1 This is an advertisement for an international football match. T
2 The match takes place in Frankfurt. F
3 The advertisement is about group travel by train. F
4 The departure is on a Sunday afternoon. F
5 The journey takes over three hours. T
6 Accommodation is in a one-star hotel. F
7 The match takes place on the second day. F
8 Most of the meals are taken at the hotel. T
9 Departure on the fourth day is at 7 p.m. F
10 The cost per person in a single room is 1035,- Marks. F

Hallo Fußballfreunde
und Leser der FRANKFURTER TAGESBLATT
Zum Länderspiel
Italien-Deutschland
am 4. Februar in Neapel
bieten wir Ihnen eine
Flugreise
vom 2. bis 5. Februar an, die das Fußballereignis mit einem Kurzurlaub im schönen Italien verbindet.

1. Tag: Abflug Sonntag 2. Februar, vormittags, von Frankfurt nach Neapel (Flugzeit 3 Std. 15 Minuten). Nach Ankunft in Neapel Transfer zum Hotel VESUVIO, einem modernen Erste-Klasse-Hotel mit herrlichem Blick auf den Golf von Neapel. Abendessen im Hotel.
2. Tag: Dieser Tag ist zu Ihrer freien Verfügung und bietet Gelegenheit zu einem Ganztagesausflug nach Pompeji, zum Vesuv und nach Neapel zum Preise von DM99,- pro Person. Abendessen im Hotel.
3. Tag: Frühstück im Hotel. Der Vormittag ist wieder zu Ihrer freien Verfügung. Nutzen Sie die Zeit, das malerische Städtchen Sorrent kennenzulernen. Mittagessen im Hotel. Im Laufe des Nachmittags Transfer von Sorrent nach Avellino zum Spiel Italien gegen Deutschland. Nach Spielende Transfer zum Hotel.
4. Tag: Frühstück im Hotel. Der Vormittag ist wieder zu Ihrer freien Verfügung. Gegen Mittag Transfer von Sorrent zum Flughafen Neapel. Abflug gegen 17 Uhr. Ankunft in Frankfurt ca. 20.30 Uhr.
Reisepreis pro Person im Doppelzimmer DM **1035,-**
Einzelzimmerzuschlag DM**114,-**

Programme, Informationen, Buchung beim Reiseveranstalter:
Reisebüro Weidmann
Josefstraße 72, 6000 Frankfurt am Main 1, Telefon 069/98 38 61, Frau Hoffmann
Weitere Buchungsstellen in Frankfurt:
Reisebüro Weidmann
Neue Koblenzer Straße 48, Telefon 069/99 47 38, und
Wagons-lits Reisebüro im Rundschau-Haus
Große Hartsheimer Straße 24-26, Telefon 069/91 94 - 377
Ein Service der Frankfurter Tagesblatt für ihre Leser

10

© Goodman-Stephens, Rogers, Briggs 1990 Published by Thomas Nelson and Sons Ltd ISBN 0-17-439251-6

SCHREIBEN

M Writing a letter about what you spend your pocket money on

Tests ability to write about how pocket money is spent.

Marking scheme:
1 mark per item, e.g.
Platten
Cassetten
Kleidung
Bücher
Zeitschriften
Bonbons
Kulis
Ohrringe etc.
Total: **8** (maximum, for communication even with error)

N Writing a letter about a holiday

Tests ability to write a penfriend letter about holiday activities, including travel, weather, meeting someone, activities and health.

Marking scheme:
Allow 1 mark per relevant statement up to a maximum of 8 plus 4 marks for overall accuracy.
e.g. Die Reise war furchtbar / Ich habe Köln besucht. / Das Wetter war toll. / Ich habe Karola (Karl)/ein Mädchen (einen Jungen) kennengelernt. / Sie (er) ist (ziemlich) groß / und hat braune Augen und schwarze Haare. / Wir sind schwimmen gegangen / und haben Tennis gespielt. / Ich habe (Eisbein) gegessen. / Es hat furchtbar geschmeckt. / Ich hatte Magenschmerzen.
Total: **8** (maximum) **+4** (maximum, for accuracy) = **12**

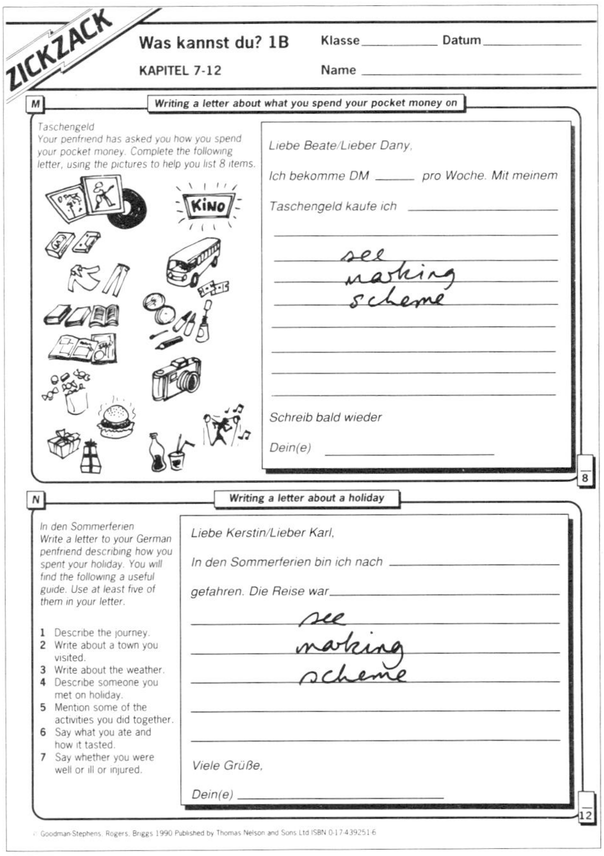

ZICKZACK

Was kannst du? 1B Klasse ____________ Datum ____________

KAPITEL 7-12 Name ____________

M **Writing a letter about what you spend your pocket money on**

Taschengeld
Your penfriend has asked you how you spend your pocket money. Complete the following letter, using the pictures to help you list 8 items.

Liebe Beate/Lieber Dany,
Ich bekomme DM ______ pro Woche. Mit meinem Taschengeld kaufe ich ______
see marking scheme
Schreib bald wieder
Dein(e) ______

8

N **Writing a letter about a holiday**

In den Sommerferien
Write a letter to your German penfriend describing how you spent your holiday. You will find the following a useful guide. Use at least five of them in your letter.

1 Describe the journey.
2 Write about a town you visited.
3 Write about the weather.
4 Describe someone you met on holiday.
5 Mention some of the activities you did together.
6 Say what you ate and how it tasted.
7 Say whether you were well or ill or injured.

Liebe Kerstin/Lieber Karl,
In den Sommerferien bin ich nach ______ gefahren. Die Reise war ______
see marking scheme
Viele Grüße,
Dein(e) ______

12

© Goodman-Stephens, Rogers, Briggs 1990 Published by Thomas Nelson and Sons Ltd ISBN 0-17-439251-6

SPRECHEN

O Speaking

Tests ability to ask and answer questions about getting into town, finding out information, saying what there is to do and making arrangements to meet.
Four different sets of pairwork materials. Two activities per pupil in pairwork.
Pupils should be given one of the roles and should then work either with a partner or with the teacher (see Introduction).

Marking scheme:
1 mark per item of information up to a maximum of 15, plus a maximum of 5 discretionary marks for fluency, accuracy, idiom/elegance of expression etc.

1A Wie komme ich / zur Stadtmitte? / Wo ist das Verkehrsamt? /Was gibt es (in der Stadt) zu sehen? / Gehen wir ins Kino? / (Um) 14 Uhr 30. / Am (Vor dem) Bahnhof./
Mit der Straßenbahn / Nummer 28 /zur Stadthalle. / Geradeaus, erste Straße rechts / und dann links (auf der linken Seite). /
Den Zoo, den Park. / Ja, gerne. / Um wieviel Uhr? /(Und) wo?
Total: **15** (maximum) **+5** (maximum) = **20**

1B Mit dem Bus Nummer 14 / zum Bahnhof / Geradeaus / und zweite Straße rechts / auf der linken Seite. / Das Schloß, den Dom (die Kathedrale). /
Ja, gerne. / Um wieviel Uhr? / (Und) wo?
Wie komme ich / zur Stadtmitte? / Wo ist die Fußgängerzone? /Was gibt es (in der Stadt) zu sehen? / Gehen wir zum Schwimmbad (schwimmen)? / (Um) 14 Uhr 20. / Am (Vor dem) Kino(center).
Total: **15** (maximum) **+5** (maximum) = **20**

2A Wie komme ich / zur Stadtmitte? / Wo ist die Bank (eine Wechselstube)? /Was gibt es (in der Stadt) zu sehen? / Gehen wir ins Eiscafé (ein Eis essen)? / (Um) 18 Uhr 30. / Am (Vor dem) Sportzentrum (Stadion)./
Mit der S-Bahn / Nummer 24 /zum (Haupt)bahnhof. / Geradeaus, / dritte Straße links / und dann die erste Straße rechts (auf der linken Seite). / Das Rathaus, das Schloß. / Ja, gerne. / Um wieviel Uhr? /(Und) wo?
Total: **15** (maximum) **+5** (maximum) = **20**

2B Mit der U-Bahn / Nummer 3 / zum Schloß / Geradeaus / und dritte Straße rechts / auf der linken Seite. / Das Museum, den Dom (die Kathedrale). /Ja, gerne. / Um wieviel Uhr? / (Und) wo?
Wie komme ich / zur Stadtmitte? / Wo ist das Kaufhaus? /Was gibt es (in der Stadt) zu sehen? / Gehen wir zum Konzert? / (Um) 17 Uhr 30. / An (Vor) der Stadthalle.
Total: **15** (maximum) **+5** (maximum) = **20**

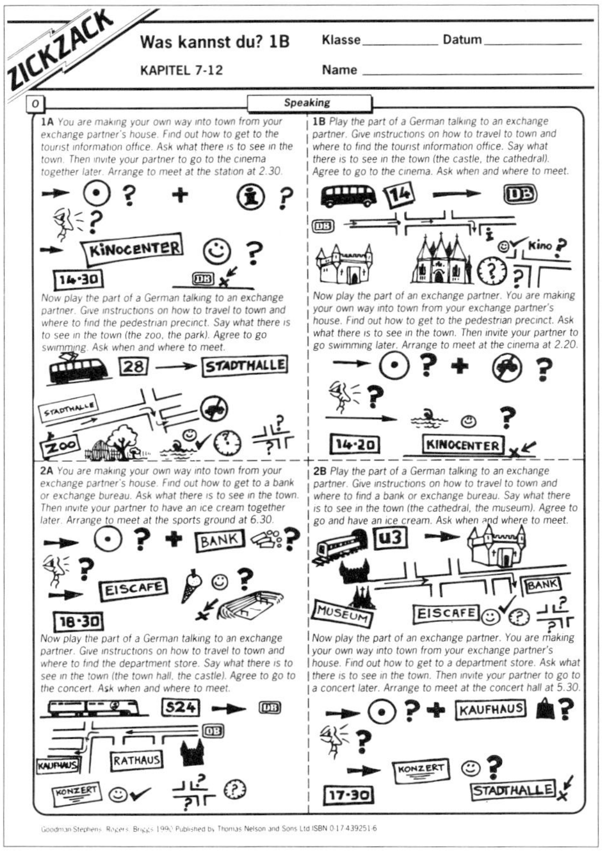
ZICKZACK
Was kannst du? 1B Klasse ________ Datum ________
KAPITEL 7-12 Name ________

O Speaking

1A You are making your own way into town from your exchange partner's house. Find out how to get to the tourist information office. Ask what there is to see in the town. Then invite your partner to go to the cinema together later. Arrange to meet at the station at 2.30.

Now play the part of a German talking to an exchange partner. Give instructions on how to travel to town and where to find the pedestrian precinct. Say what there is to see in the town (the zoo, the park). Agree to go swimming. Ask when and where to meet.

1B Play the part of a German talking to an exchange partner. Give instructions on how to travel to town and where to find the tourist information office. Say what there is to see in the town (the castle, the cathedral). Agree to go to the cinema. Ask when and where to meet.

Now play the part of an exchange partner. You are making your own way into town from your exchange partner's house. Find out how to get to the pedestrian precinct. Ask what there is to see in the town. Then invite your partner to go swimming later. Arrange to meet at the cinema at 2.20.

2A You are making your own way into town from your exchange partner's house. Find out how to get to a bank or exchange bureau. Ask what there is to see in the town. Then invite your partner to have an ice cream together later. Arrange to meet at the sports ground at 6.30.

Now play the part of a German talking to an exchange partner. Give instructions on how to travel to town and where to find the department store. Say what there is to see in the town (the town hall, the castle). Agree to go to the concert. Ask when and where to meet.

2B Play the part of a German talking to an exchange partner. Give instructions on how to travel to town and where to find a bank or exchange bureau. Say what there is to see in the town (the cathedral, the museum). Agree to go and have an ice cream. Ask when and where to meet.

Now play the part of an exchange partner. You are making your own way into town from your exchange partner's house. Find out how to get to a department store. Ask what there is to see in the town. Then invite your partner to go to a concert later. Arrange to meet at the concert hall at 5.30.

Goodman-Stephens, Rogers, Briggs 1990 Published by Thomas Nelson and Sons Ltd ISBN 0-17-439251-6

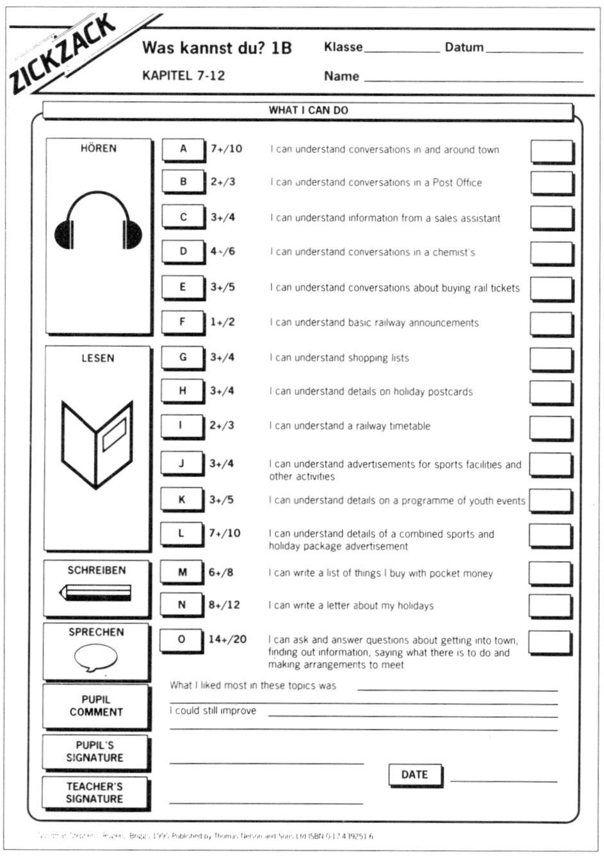
ZICKZACK
Was kannst du? 1B Klasse ________ Datum ________
KAPITEL 7-12 Name ________

WHAT I CAN DO

HÖREN	A	7+/10	I can understand conversations in and around town	
	B	2+/3	I can understand conversations in a Post Office	
	C	3+/4	I can understand information from a sales assistant	
	D	4+/6	I can understand conversations in a chemist's	
	E	3+/5	I can understand conversations about buying rail tickets	
	F	1+/2	I can understand basic railway announcements	
LESEN	G	3+/4	I can understand shopping lists	
	H	3+/4	I can understand details on holiday postcards	
	I	2+/3	I can understand a railway timetable	
	J	3+/4	I can understand advertisements for sports facilities and other activities	
	K	3+/5	I can understand details on a programme of youth events	
	L	7+/10	I can understand details of a combined sports and holiday package advertisement	
SCHREIBEN	M	6+/8	I can write a list of things I buy with pocket money	
	N	8+/12	I can write a letter about my holidays	
SPRECHEN	O	14+/20	I can ask and answer questions about getting into town, finding out information, saying what there is to do and making arrangements to meet	

PUPIL COMMENT
What I liked most in these topics was ________
I could still improve ________

PUPIL'S SIGNATURE ________

TEACHER'S SIGNATURE ________ DATE ________

Goodman-Stephens, Rogers, Briggs 1990 Published by Thomas Nelson and Sons Ltd ISBN 0-17-439251-6

Was kannst du? 1B — Kapitel 7

Pupil's Name	A	B	C	D	Total	E	F	Total	G	H	Total	Comment
	4/6	3/4	2/3	6/8	15/21	6/9	3/5	9/14	3/5	6/10	33/50	
1												
2												
3												
4												
5												
6												
7												
8												
9												
10												
11												
12												
13												
14												
15												
16												
17												
18												
19												
20												
21												
22												
23												
24												
25												
26												
27												
28												
29												

Was kannst du? 1B — Kapitel 8

Pupil's Name	A	B	C	Total	D	E	F	Total	G	H	Total	Comment
	4/6	3/4	4/6	11/16	3/4	4/6	6/8	13/18	4/6	6/10	34/50	
1												
2												
3												
4												
5												
6												
7												
8												
9												
10												
11												
12												
13												
14												
15												
16												
17												
18												
19												
20												
21												
22												
23												
24												
25												
26												
27												
28												
29												
30												

© Goodman-Stephens, Rogers, Briggs 1990 Published by Thomas Nelson and Sons Ltd ISBN 0-17-439251-6

Was kannst du? 1B — Kapitel 9

Pupil's Name	A	B	C	D	Total	E	F	Total	G	H	Total	Comment
	4/5	3/5	4/6	3/4	14/20	5/7	5/7	10/14	4/6	6/10	34/50	
1												
2												
3												
4												
5												
6												
7												
8												
9												
10												
11												
12												
13												
14												
15												
16												
17												
18												
19												
20												
21												
22												
23												
24												
25												
26												
27												
28												
29												
30												

Was kannst du? 1B — Kapitel 7 - 9

Pupil's Name	A	B	C	D	Total	E	F	G	H	Total	I	J	Total	K	Total
	6/8	7/9	7/9	7/9	27/35	3/4	7/10	5/7	3/4	18/25	7/10	7/10	14/20	14/20	73/100
1															
2															
3															
4															
5															
6															
7															
8															
9															
10															
11															
12															
13															
14															
15															
16															
17															
18															
19															
20															
21															
22															
23															
24															
25															
26															
27															
28															
29															
30															

© Goodman-Stephens, Rogers, Briggs 1990 Published by Thomas Nelson and Sons Ltd ISBN 0-17-439251-6

Was kannst du? 1B — Kapitel 10

Pupil's Name	A	B	C	D	Total	E	F	Total	G	H	Total	Comment
	4/6	4/6	2/3	3/5	13/20	6/9	3/5	9/14	4/6	6/10	32/50	
1												
2												
3												
4												
5												
6												
7												
8												
9												
10												
11												
12												
13												
14												
15												
16												
17												
18												
19												
20												
21												
22												
23												
24												
25												
26												
27												
28												
29												
30												

Was kannst du? 1B — Kapitel 11

Pupil's Name	A	B	C	Total	D	E	F	Total	G	H	Total	Comment
	3/4	6/8	3/4	12/16	5/7	4/6	3/5	12/18	4/6	6/10	34/50	
1												
2												
3												
4												
5												
6												
7												
8												
9												
10												
11												
12												
13												
14												
15												
16												
17												
18												
19												
20												
21												
22												
23												
24												
25												
26												
27												
28												
29												
30												

© Goodman-Stephens, Rogers, Briggs 1990 Published by Thomas Nelson and Sons Ltd ISBN 0-17-439251-6

Was kannst du? 1B — Kapitel 12

Pupil's Name	A	B	C	Total	D	E	Total	G	H	Total	Comment
	7/9	4/6	3/5	14/20	4/6	6/8	10/14	4/6	6/10	34/50	
1											
2											
3											
4											
5											
6											
7											
8											
9											
10											
11											
12											
13											
14											
15											
16											
17											
18											
19											
20											
21											
22											
23											
24											
25											
26											
27											
28											
29											
30											

Was kannst du? 1B — Kapitel 7 - 12

Pupil's Name	A	B	C	D	E	F	Total	G	H	I	J	K	L	Total	M	N	Total	O	Total
	7/10	2/3	3/4	4/6	3/5	1/2	20/30	3/4	3/4	2/3	3/4	3/5	7/10	21/30	6/8	8/12	14/20	14/20	69/100
1																			
2																			
3																			
4																			
5																			
6																			
7																			
8																			
9																			
10																			
11																			
12																			
13																			
14																			
15																			
16																			
17																			
18																			
19																			
20																			
21																			
22																			
23																			
24																			
25																			
26																			
27																			
28																			
29																			
30																			

© Goodman-Stephens, Rogers, Briggs 1990 Published by Thomas Nelson and Sons Ltd ISBN 0-17-439251-6

Notes

Practical Pre-School

CW01652344

Planning for Learning through All About Me

Rachel Sparks Linfield and Penny Coltman Illustrated by Cathy Hughes

Contents

Published by Step Forward Publishing Limited
35 Park Court, Park Street, Leamington Spa CV32 4QN Tel: 01926 420046
Step Forward Publishing Limited 1999
All rights reserved. No part of this publication may be reproduced, stored in a retrieval system, or transmitted by any means, electronic, mechanical, photocopied or otherwise, without the prior permission of the publisher.
Planning for Learning through All About Me ISBN: 1 902438 13 2

Making plans

Why plan?

The purpose of planning is to make sure that all children enjoy a broad and balanced curriculum. All planning should be useful. Plans are working documents which you spend time preparing, but which should later repay your efforts. Try to be concise. This will help you in finding information quickly when you need it.

Long-term plans

Preparing a long-term plan, which maps out the curriculum during a year or even two, will help you to ensure that you are providing a variety of activities and are meeting statutory requirements of the Early Learning Goals (1999).

Your long-term plan need not be detailed. Divide the time period over which you are planning into fairly equal sections, such as half terms. Choose a topic for each section. Young children benefit from making links between the new ideas they encounter so as you select each topic, think about the time of year in which you plan to do it. A topic about minibeasts will not be very successful in November!

Although each topic will address all the areas of learning, some could focus on a specific area. For example, a topic on All About Me lends itself well to activities relating to personal, social and emotional development and knowledge and understanding of the world. Another topic might particularly encourage the appreciation of stories. Try to make sure that you provide a variety of topics in your long-term plans.

Autumn 1	All About Me
Autumn 2	Autumn/Christmas
Spring 1	Fairy Stories
Spring 2	Colour
Summer 1	Toys
Summer 2	Minibeasts

Medium-term plans

Medium-term plans will outline the contents of a topic in a little more detail. One way to start this process is by brainstorming on a large piece of paper. Work with your team writing down all the activities you can think of which are relevant to the topic. As you do this it may become clear that some activities go well together. Think about dividing them into themes. All About Me, for example, has themes such as 'Hands', 'Looking', 'Listening' and 'Faces'.

At this stage it is helpful to make a chart. Write the theme ideas down the side of the chart and put a different area of learning at the top of each column. Now you can insert your brainstormed ideas and quickly see where there are gaps. As you complete the chart take account of children's earlier experiences and provide opportunities for them to progress.

Refer back to the Early Learning Goals document and check that you have addressed as many different aspects of it as you can. Once all your medium-term plans are complete make sure that there are no neglected areas.

Day-to-day plans

The plans you make for each day will outline aspects such as:

- resources needed;
- the way in which you might introduce activities;
- the organisation of adult help;
- size of the group;
- timing.

Making plans

Identify the learning which each activity is intended to promote. Make a note of any assessments or observations which you are likely to carry out. On your plans make notes of which activities were particularly successful, or any changes you would make another time.

A final note

Planning should be seen as flexible. Not all groups meet every day, and not all children attend every day. Any part of the plan can be used independently, stretched over a longer period or condensed to meet the needs of any group. You will almost certainly adapt the activities as children respond to them in different ways and bring their own ideas, interests and enthusiasms. The important thing is to ensure that the children are provided with a varied and enjoyable curriculum which meets their individual developing needs.

Using the book

- Collect or prepare suggested resources as listed on page 21.
- Read the section which outlines links to the Early Learning Goals (pages 4 - 7) and explains the rationale for the topic of All About Me.
- For each weekly theme two activities are described in detail as an example to help you in your planning and preparation. Key vocabulary, questions and learning opportunities are identified.
- The skills chart on page 23 will help you to see at a glance which aspects of children's development are being addressed as a focus each week.
- As children take part in the All About Me topic activities, their learning will progress. 'Collecting evidence' on page 22 explains how you might monitor children's achievements.
- Find out on page 20 how the topic can be brought together in a grand finale involving parents, children and friends.
- There is additional material to support the working partnership of families and children in the form of a 'Home links' page, and a photocopiable 'Parent's page' found at the back of the book.

It is important to appreciate that the ideas presented in this book will only be a part of your planning. Many activities which will be taking place as routine in your group may not be mentioned. For example, it is assumed that sand, dough, water, puzzles, floor toys and large scale apparatus are part of the ongoing pre-school experience. Many groups will also be able to provide access to computers and other aspects of information and communication technology. Role play areas, stories, rhymes and singing, and group discussion times are similarly assumed to be happening each week although they may not be a focus for described activities.

Using the Early Learning Goals

Having decided on your topic and made your medium-term plans you can use the Early Learning Goals to highlight the key learning opportunities your activities will address. The Early Learning Goals are split into six areas: Personal, Social and Emotional Development, Language and Literacy, Mathematics, Knowledge and Understanding of the World, Physical Development and Creative Development. Do not expect each of your topics to cover every goal but your long-term plans should allow for each child to work towards all of the goals.

The following section highlights parts of the Early Learning Goals document in point form to show what children are expected to be able to do by the time they enter Year 1 in each area of learning. These points will be used throughout this book to show how activities for a topic on All About Me link to these expectations. For example, Personal, Social and Emotional development point 8 is 'work as part of a group or class taking turns'. Activities suggested which provide the opportunity for children to do this will have the reference PS8. This will enable you to see which parts of the Early Learning Goals are covered in a given week and plan for areas to be revisited and developed.

In addition you can ensure that activities offer variety in the outcomes to be encountered. Often a similar activity may be carried out to achieve different outcomes. For example, during this topic children make an eye colour bar chart. They will be saying and using number names but they will also be using language such as 'more' and 'fewer', collaborating and learning to work together. It is important therefore that activities have clearly defined learning outcomes so that these may be emphasised during the activity and for recording purposes.

Personal, Social and Emotional Development (PS)

This area of learning incorporates attitudes, skills and understanding and is a pre-condition for children's success in all other learning. The goals include children's personal, social, emotional, moral and spiritual development and the establishment of good attitudes to their learning.

By the end of the reception year most children should be:

PS1 confident to try things, initiate ideas and speak in a group

PS2 able to maintain attention, concentrate and sit still

PS3 interested, excited and motivated to learn

PS4 aware of their own needs, views and feelings and sensitive to the needs, views and feelings of others

PS5 respectful of their own cultures and beliefs and those of other people

PS6 responsive to significant experiences showing a range of feelings including joy, awe, wonder and sorrow

They should be able to:

PS7 form good relationships with peers and adults

PS8 work as a part of a group or class taking turns and sharing fairly; understanding that there need to be agreed values and codes of behaviour for groups of people, including adults and children, to work harmoniously

PS9 understand what is right, what is wrong and why

PS10 dress and undress independently and manage their own personal hygiene

PS11 select and use activities and resources independently

PS12 consider the consequences of their words and actions for themselves and others

PS13 understand that people have different needs, views, cultures and beliefs which need to be treated with respect

The topic of All About Me offers many opportunities for children's personal, social and emotional development. Time spent discussing the importance of various body parts will encourage children to speak in a group, to be interested and to consider consequences. By playing circle games children will learn to take turns and to understand the need for agreed codes of behaviour. Many of the areas outlined above, though, will be covered on an almost incidental basis as children carry out the activities described in this book for the other areas of learning. During undirected free choice times they will be developing independence (PS11) whilst any small group activity which involves working with an adult will help children to work towards PS7.

Language and Literacy (L)

These goals are in line with the National Literacy Strategy.

Speaking and Listening

By the end of the reception year, most children should be able to:

L1 use language to imagine and recreate roles and experiences

L2 use talk to organise, sequence and clarify thinking, ideas, feelings and events

L3 sustain attentive listening, responding to what they have heard by relevant comments, questions or actions

L4 interact with others negotiating plans and activities and taking turns in conversation

L5 extend their vocabulary exploring the meaning and sounds of new words

L6 retell narratives in the correct sequence drawing on the language pattern of stories

L7 speak clearly and audibly with confidence and control and show awareness of the listener, for example by their use of conventions such as greetings, 'please' and 'thank you'

Reading

By the end of reception most children should be able to:

L8 hear and say initial and final sounds in words and short vowel sounds within words

L9 link letters and sounds, naming and sounding all letters of the alphabet

L10 read a range of familiar and common words and simple sentences independently

L11 show understanding of elements of stories such as main character, sequence of events, opening and how information can be found in non-fiction texts, to answer questions about where, who, why and how

Writing

By the end of reception most children should be able to:

L12 hold a pencil correctly, and form recognisable letters, most of which are correctly formed

L13 use their phonic knowledge to write simple regular words and make phonetically plausible attempts at more complex words

L14 write their own names and labels and form sentences, sometimes using punctuation

L15 attempt writing for various purposes, using features of different forms such as lists, stories, instructions

The activities suggested for the theme of All About Me include several which are based on well-known, quality picture books and stories. They allow children to enjoy listening to the books and to respond in a variety of ways to what they hear, reinforcing and extending their vocabularies. Throughout the topic opportunities are described in which children are encouraged to explore the sounds of words, to use descriptive vocabulary and to see some of their ideas recorded in both pictures and words. As children become more aware of their hands, their eyes and their ears they are encouraged to use their senses during story times, role play situations and book making activities.

Mathematics (M)

These goals reflect the key objectives in the National Numeracy Strategy.

By the end of reception most children should be able to:

M1 say and use number names in order in familiar contexts

M2 count reliably up to ten everyday objects;

M3 recognise numerals 1 to 9

M4 use language such as 'more' or 'less', 'greater' or 'smaller', 'heavier' or 'lighter' to compare two numbers or quantities

M5 in practical activities and discussion begin to use the vocabulary involved in adding and subtracting

M6 find one more or one less than a number from one to ten

M7 begin to relate addition to combining two groups of objects and subtraction to 'taking away'

M8 talk about, recognise and recreate simple patterns

M9 use language such as 'circle' or 'bigger' to describe the shape and size of solids and flat shapes

M10 use everyday words to describe position

M11 use developing mathematical ideas and methods to solve practical problems

The theme of All About Me provides a meaningful context for mathematical activities. Children are given the opportunity to count people, hands and facial features and to begin to develop language for addition and subtraction. Hands and feet are used as non-standard units for measuring. There are opportunities for children to explore shape, size and position as they compare ears and hands whilst the 'Listening week' allows children to play a variety of lotto type number games.

Knowledge and Understanding of the World (K)

These goals provide a foundation for scientific, technological, historical and geographical learning.

By the end of reception most children should be able to:

K1 investigate objects and materials by using all of their senses as appropriate

K2 find out about and identify some features of, living things, objects and events they observe

K3 look closely at similarities, differences, patterns and change

K4 ask questions about why things happen and how things work

K5 build and construct with a wide range of objects, selecting appropriate resources and adapting their work where necessary

K6 select tools and techniques they need to shape, assemble and join the materials they are using

K7 find out about and identify the uses of technology in their everyday lives and use computers and programmed toys to support their learning

K8 find out about past and present events in their own lives, and those of their families and other people they know

K9 observe find out about and identify features in the place where they live and the natural world

K10 find out about their environment and talk about those features they like and dislike

The topic of All About Me offers many opportunities for children to make observations, to ask questions and to compare. They can explore the differences and similarities in eyes, hands, feet and ears. By making jointed bodies and a full sized poster of a child they will become more aware of their own bodies and how the various parts are positioned. By recording finger prints with chalk/ink and hand prints in clay, and by making face masks they will be encouraged to notice details and features whilst at the same time gain a greater understanding of the properties of materials.

Physical Development (PD)

By the end of reception most children should be able to:

PD1 move with confidence, imagination and in safety

PD2 move with control and co-ordination

PD3 show awareness of space, of themselves and of others

PD4 recognise the importance of keeping healthy and those things which contribute to this

PD5 recognise the changes that happen to their bodies when they are active

PD6 use a range of small and large equipment

PD7 travel around, under, over and through balancing and climbing equipment

PD8 handle tools, objects, construction and malleable materials safely with increasing control.

Activities such as playing with playdough and construction toys with small pieces will offer experience of PD8. Through pretending to be spies in disguise, shadowing a person or by playing 'Keeper of the Keys' children will have the opportunity to develop PD1 and 2. As children learn how to warm up before active games they will become more aware of how their bodies change. As children are encouraged to notice what their bodies can do there are many opportunities for aiming, balancing and movement activities.

Creative Development (C)

By the end of reception most children should be able to:

C1 explore colour, texture, shape, form and space in two and three dimensions

C2 listen attentively to and explore how sounds can be made louder/quieter, faster/slower, longer/shorter, higher/lower and recognise patterns in music, movement and dance

C3 respond in a variety of ways to what they see, hear, smell, touch and feel

C4 use their imagination in art and design, music, dance, drama, stories and play

C5 express and communicate their ideas, thoughts and feelings by using a widening range of materials, suitable tools, drama, movement, designing and making, and a variety of songs and instruments

During this topic children will experience working with a variety of materials as they make collages of faces and clown puppets. They will be able to develop their skills of painting and colour mixing as they paint self-portraits and so work towards C1 and 4. A number of songs which have body parts in them have been suggested which could also have actions and percussion added, so allowing children to use their imagination in music. Throughout all the activities children are encouraged to talk about what they see and feel as they communicate their ideas in painting, collage work and role play.

Week 1

Bits and pieces

Personal, Social and Emotional Development

- During circle time show children how to roll a ball gently to a friend. On receiving the ball the child says 'My name is ______ and with my * I can _______.' The * should be a body part such as 'with my hands I can draw'. (PS2, 8)
- Make a collection of objects familiar to the children which can be used in a foot feely box. Children should take it in turns to feel an object with their feet and describe it to the rest of the group. After the game has finished, talk about whether it is easier to use feet or hands for this activity and why. (PS1, 8)
- Use a large picture of a child as the focus for a discussion on body parts and how useful they are. For example, the nose can smell and act as a filter for dust and smoke particles. (PS1, 2, 6)

Language and Literacy

- Read *Funnybones* by Janet and Allan Ahlberg (Picture Lions). Talk about skeletons and how they support our bodies. Re-read the story, encouraging children to join in. (L2, 3)
- Help children to write name labels for a display of self-portraits. (L12, 14)
- Take a photograph of each child. Mount each one on a large sheet of card and ask each child to complete a page about themselves for a big book. Each page should give the child's name, their age, what they like to do and any other details which fit in with the body 'bits and pieces' theme. (L12)

Mathematics

- Help children to draw round their feet. Compare feet sizes and use them as a non-standard measure for a variety of lengths. (M4)
- Use *Funnybones* by Janet and Allan Ahlberg (Picture Lions) as the stimulus for comparing sizes of dolls and teddies and to reinforce associated language for size. (M4)
- Play a beetle drive type game in which children throw a dice and each number corresponds to a part of the body. (M3)

Knowledge and Understanding of the World

- Draw around a child. Label different parts of the body (see activity opposite). (K2)
- Make skeletons from pieces of white paper straws mounted on black paper. (K5)
- To reinforce names of body parts make jointed people from card pieces with brass fasteners for the joints. (K2, 5)

Physical Development

- Play 'Simon says', emphasising names of body parts in the instructions. (PD 1, 2)
- Experiment with travelling and balancing using different body parts. (PD1, 2, 7)
- Play with balls and compare the way they move when they are thrown and kicked. Which parts of our bodies can we use to make the ball move? (PD6)

Creative Development

- Sing 'Heads, shoulders, knees and toes'. (C4)
- Paint self-portraits (see activity opposite). (C1)
- Explore which parts of the body can be used to make sounds to accompany songs. Children could clap, tap, click fingers, sniff, whistle, stamp, slap thighs, tap teeth, and so on. Encourage children to explore how the sounds can be made louder, quieter, faster and slower. (C2, 5)

Activity: Self-portraits

Learning opportunity: Painting based on close observation.

Early Learning Goal: Creative Development. Children will explore colour and shape in two dimensions.

Resources: Ready-mixed paints in a range of colours so that children can pick the appropriate skin, hair and eye colours; plastic mirrors; photographs of people familiar to the group.

Key vocabulary: Names of colours, parts of the body, portrait.

Organisation: Small group.

What to do:

Show children the photographs. Who are in the photos? What are the people wearing? What colours are their hair? Show children the paints. Pick one person in the photos. Ask the group which paint they would choose for that person's hair if they were to do a portrait. What would they use for the skin? Explain to the children that they are going to paint self-portraits. Talk about the need to choose colours carefully so that everyone will be able to recognise them from the pictures. As children paint, encourage them to notice where eyes should be positioned, and how arms and legs are placed in relationship to their bodies.

Activity: Labelling body parts

Learning opportunity: Recognising and labelling parts of the body.

Early Learning Goal: Knowledge and Understanding of the World. Children will find out about and identify features of living things.

Resources: Large plain paper as long as a child; thick, black wax crayon; labels of the body parts.

Key vocabulary: Eye, ear, mouth, nose, head, arm, neck, elbow, hand, shoulder, tummy/stomach, waist, knee, foot, finger, toe (**Note:** The number and type of words to be used will vary from group to group.)

Organisation: Small group sitting on the floor.

What to do:

Introduce the activity with a quick game of 'Point to your .....' in order to assess which body part names children are already familiar with. Explain to the group that they are going to make a large poster to teach people the names for parts of the body. Show the children some of the labels. Can anyone recognise any of the words? What sounds do the words begin with? Choose a child who is wearing shorts or trousers to lie down on the large piece of paper and draw round them with the wax crayon. Ask the children to help you stick the labels on to the poster. Mount the poster at floor height.

Display

Mount the body poster at floor height. As the weeks progress put out other labels for children to add to the body. Make a track of the feet used for measuring going to the body as if the body has walked all over the wall. Display the skeletons on a board near a table containing other books in the *Funnybones* series.

Cut around the portraits and mount on black sugar paper. Display the portraits against a background of a play area as if the children are enjoying a playtime together.

Week 2

Handy week

Personal, Social and Emotional Development

- During circle time play games in which children pass on claps of differing numbers and rhythms. Encourage children to listen and to take turns. (PS2, 8)
- Talk about the importance of washing hands before eating. Encourage children to become independent. (PS10)
- Talk about why people shake hands. Discuss which hand is shaken and reinforce 'right' and 'left'. For a week encourage children to shake hands with you each day when they arrive or before going home. (PS12)

Language and Literacy

- Clap children's names and encourage them to recognise their own and those of friends. (L3)
- Prepare a feely bag of objects found in the classroom. Ask children to take it in turns to describe what they feel. (L3)
- Draw around children's hands and help them to fill their hands with either words or pictures of things they can do with their hands. Once full, cut them out. (L12, 15)
- Use fingers to enjoy practising early hand writing patterns in trays of coloured sand. (L12)

Mathematics

- Use a variety of finger rhymes to reinforce numbers to five. (M1)
- Use ready mixed paint to make a hand print for each child. When dry, cut around the prints and compare the sizes. Use the prints as leaves and ask the children to stick them on a large painted tree. Encourage the use of positional language as the children talk about where their 'leaves' have been stuck. (M4, 10)
- Measure lengths in hand spans. (M4)
- Play the handy estimation game (see activity opposite). (M4, 7)

Knowledge and Understanding of the World

- Make thumb prints. Use magnifiers to explore the different patterns and see how they are all different (see activity opposite). (K2, 3)
- Provide a range of materials for children to choose from to make their own models. As they work, encourage them to talk about what their hands are doing. (K5, 6)
- Compare hands. Help children to notice differences in palm lines, nail colours and sizes. Make a hand print in clay or dough. (K3)

Physical Development

- Encourage the development of fine motor skills by using construction toys with small pieces. (PD6)
- Play catching and throwing games. (PD6)
- Explore what hands can do to squeeze, roll and flatten playdough. (PD8)

Creative Development

- Use finger paints to make prints with fingers. Add lines and dots to turn the prints into small creatures. Encourage children to talk about their creatures. Where do they live? What can they do? What do they eat? (C4)
- Sing favourite songs and take it in turns to clap the rhythm. (C5)
- On black paper draw around a child's hand with white chalk several times so that the shapes touch and form a pattern. Ask children to choose three colours with which to paint their hand pattern. (C1)

Activity: Handy estimation game

Learning opportunity: Mathematics. Estimating and counting numbers to ten.

Early Learning Goal: Children will count reliably up to ten objects and use language such as 'more' and 'less'.

Resources: A basket of small objects (for example, Unifix cubes) such that a child's handful would be no more than ten; number cards for numerals to nine.

Key vocabulary: Numbers to ten, more, less than, fewer.

Organisation: Small group.

What to do:

Invite a child to pick a handful of cubes from the basket. Ask the child to count how many there are. Ask another child to try and pick out a handful which has about the same number of cubes in it. How many are there? Is it the same number? Are there more/fewer cubes in the second handful? Continue this activity until all children have had a chance to be both the first picker and the second.

Next, show children a number card. Ask them to try to pick out quickly from the basket exactly the same number of cubes. Encourage children to do this by estimating rather than by counting. If appropriate, extend the game by asking children to pick up more/fewer cubes. On further occasions the language of addition/subtraction can also be used.

Activity: Thumb prints

Learning opportunity: Observing and describing thumb prints.

Early Learning Goal: Knowledge and Understanding of the World. Children will identify features of thumbs and will look closely at similarities and differences.

Resources: Wide sticky tape; scissors; white chalk; magnifiers; postcard sized pieces of black sugar paper.

Key vocabulary: Thumb, print.

Organisation: Small group.

What to do:

Explain to the children that everyone has thumb prints and that everybody's print is different. Ask the group to look at their thumb prints with the magnifiers. What can they see? Hand out pieces of white chalk and show the children how to cover their thumb prints with chalk dust. Being careful not to finger the sticky part of the tape, cut a piece and hold it firmly at each end. Ask a child to place their thumb in the centre on the sticky side and lift it off. Stick the tape on a piece of black sugar paper and let the child examine it. Repeat the sticky tape exercise for each child's left and right thumb, remembering to name each one. Help children to notice the different patterns and to draw what they see on white paper.

Display

Paint two large tree trunks with branches (let the children help you). Ask them where they want to stick their hand prints and handy words. Encourage them to explain the positions they choose rather than letting them simply point. On a nearby table place the clay hand prints and the thumb prints with two magnifiers.

Week 3

Listening week

Personal, Social and Emotional Development

- During circle time talk about the importance of being a good listener. Emphasise that in order to show we are listening to someone we need to look at them as they speak. (PS2, 4)
- Tell the traditional tale of 'The boy who cried wolf'. Talk about the boy and why he should not have cried for help when he did not need it. (PS9)
- Make a collection of precious objects which make a sound, such as a china bell, a baby's rattle and a bunch of keys. Explain to the children why each object is precious. Talk about the need to handle precious objects with care. Do the group think they can pass them around so carefully that they will not make a sound? (PS4)

Language and Literacy

- Read *Peace at Last* by Jill Murphy (Macmillan Children's Books). Write a group version with new sounds (see activity opposite). (L6, 15)
- Play Chinese whispers but instead of the final person saying the word they have heard, ask them to say the name of the letter or sound it begins with. (L3, 8)
- Begin a word bank of words which rhyme with 'ear'. (L5)

Mathematics

- Play number lotto and other games where children need to listen to instructions. (M1)
- Cut out a variety of different sizes and shapes of ears from card. Ask children to sort the ears according to shape and then to arrange each set in order of size. (M9)
- Provide each child with a small drum or shaker. Use these for counting activities. Ask children to shake/hit a given number of times. Ask them to count your taps/hits and to copy. Can they do one more hit? (M1, 6)

Knowledge and Understanding of the World

- Make a tape recording of each child saying 'Good morning'. Play the tape to the children. Can they identify their own voice? How does it compare to their normal speaking voice? (K3)
- Go on a sound detecting walk. (K2)
- Use a xylophone or glockenspiel to explore high and low notes. Invite children to design and make their own musical instruments and to describe the sounds they make. (K3, 6)

Physical Development

- Play games in which a whistle is blown or a drum is tapped a certain number of times to signify an action, such as two taps means jump, one tap means hop and three taps means sit down. (PD1, 2, 3)
- Play 'The keeper of the keys' (see activity opposite). (PD2)
- Play musical statues, encouraging children to move in time with music and to stand still as soon as the music stops. Instead of asking children to sit out if they move after the music ends, praise those who remain still. (PD2, 3)

Creative Development

- Ask children to listen to extracts of *Peter and the Wolf*. Encourage children to make up dances to the music. (C5)
- Read *Mr Little's New Car* by Richard Fowler (Mammoth) or a similar book to which children can add percussion for sound effects. Tape record the story and sounds. Later use the tape as the stimulus for a music and movement session. (C4)
- Sing and make up actions for the song 'Do your ears hang low?' in *Okki-tokki-unga Action Songs for Children* (A & C Black). (C5)

Activity: Peace at last

Learning opportunity: Collaborating to write and make a big book based on *Peace at Last.*

Early Learning Goal: Language and Literacy. Children will retell narratives and attempt to write a story.

Resources: *Peace at Last* (big book version if possible); large pieces of card or stiff paper for book pages; a variety of crayons, pencils and felt pens; a flip chart; a favourite doll or teddy owned by the group.

Key vocabulary: Vocabulary within *Peace at Last,* title, author.

Organisation: Whole group.

What to do:

At the beginning of the week read *Peace at Last* to the group. To introduce the writing of a big book, ask children to help retell the *Peace at Last* story by using the pictures in the book. Draw attention to details in the pictures and encourage all children to join in repeating phrases such as 'I can't stand this!'

Talk to children about the noises they hear when they go to bed at night. Can they describe the sounds? Explain that together they are going to write a story about the group's doll/teddy who finds it difficult to get to sleep. Discuss who else might be in the story.

On the flip chart begin to write the new story, writing just one sentence per page. Encourage children to suggest their own ideas as well as those in the book by Jill Murphy. Once the story has been written, read it back to the children. Do they like it? Are there any changes that could be made to improve it? Once children are satisfied, give each child one page to illustrate and divide into smaller groups.

Activity: The keeper of the keys

Learning opportunity: Moving quietly with control. Collaborating to play a circle game.

Early Learning Goal: Physical Development. Children will move with control and co-ordination.

Resources: Large bunch of keys.

Key vocabulary: Quietly, slowly, keys, blindfold, guard.

Organisation: Whole group.

What to do:

After a warm-up activity which encourages children to listen, arrange them sitting on the floor in a large circle. Show everyone the keys. Ask the children to shut their eyes and listen to the sound the keys make as they are picked up. Ask if anyone thinks they could pick them up without making a sound. Allow two children to demonstrate.

Pick a child to be 'The keeper of the keys' and to sit on a chair placed in the middle of the circle. Explain that the keeper has to guard the keys. If they hear someone approaching the keys they should point to where the sound is coming from. If they point at the person they have saved the keys. If someone manages to take the keys back to their place without being pointed at, the keys are lost. The keeper may only point five times. Explain that when everyone is sitting silently you will pick someone to try and take the keys.

Talk about the need to sit very still and, when picked, to move very slowly and quietly. When everyone has understood the game, blindfold the keeper and play until all children have had the chance to be either the keeper or the taker. The game can be extended by having more than one taker at a time and by reducing the number of points allowed to three.

Display

Display the instruments which children have made on a table. On another table put out a selection of instruments along with *Mr Little's Noisy Car, Peace at Last,* the group's own big book and other well-known picture books. Encourage pairs of children to use the instruments during independent activity times to make sound effects for the stories.

Week 4

Looking week

Personal, Social and Emotional Development

- Encourage children to take turns whilst playing 'I spy'. Clues could be by colour, initial sound or position. (PS8)
- Play blindfold games. (PS6, 8)

Language and Literacy

- Share books such as *I Spy Schooldays: a Book of Picture Riddles* by Walter Wick and Jean Marzollo (Scholastic) or *1001 Things to Spot on the Farm* by Gillian Doherty (Usborne) which encourage children to look closely at the pictures, to use descriptive vocabulary and to discuss with others as objects are found or cannot be seen. (L4)
- Encourage children to practise letter formation by making eye charts for the role play area. (L12)
- Read *If At First You Do Not See* by Ruth Brown. Talk about what is in each picture. Does everyone see the same things? (L2)

Mathematics

- Count how many children have each eye colour. Display the results as a bar chart (see activity opposite) (M1, 4)
- Provide each child with a book made from two pieces of A4 paper folded in half. On each page write a number from one to five. Give each child a number of magazines/catalogues which have people in them and ask the children to cut out faces and stick the given number on each page. Use the books for counting and for introducing the idea of doubles - if there are two faces on a page there will be four eyes or two pairs. (M2, 3)
- Help children to make spectacles for a teddy bear out of pipe cleaners and talk about the shapes used for the eye pieces. Can children make square eye pieces? What would triangular ones look like? (M9)

Knowledge and Understanding of the World

- Invite an adult who wears glasses to talk to the group about their glasses and what happens when they go to the optician. (K8)
- Talk about eyes and what eyelashes and eyebrows are for. Encourage children to notice the variety in eye colours and that all eyes are different even though many people have blue, brown, grey and green eyes. (K2, 3)
- Enjoy playing with safe kaleidoscopes and periscopes. (K1, 4)

Physical Development

- Talk about the importance of looking when playing with balls and bats. Allow free play, encouraging children always to keep their eyes on the ball. (PD6)
- Play a variety of aiming games such as skittles or throwing bean bags or balls into hoops or buckets. (PD6)
- Play a game where a coloured card is used to signify an action such as jump, walk or hop. Encourage children to keep a close eye on the colour card and to change their action immediately the cards have been changed. (PD2, 3)

Creative Development

- During free painting, encourage children to look closely at shapes and colours. (C4)
- Cut out pairs of spectacle frames from card and let children decorate them with sequins and other shiny and bright materials. Put them on sale in the optician role play area. (C1)
- Set up the role play area as an optician's with letter charts. Invite children to test friends', dolls' and teddy bears' eyes (see activity below). (C4)

Activity: Eye colour bar chart

Learning opportunity: Collaborating to make a bar chart and comparing the number of children with different eye colours.

Early Learning Goal: Mathematics. Children will say and use number names and use language such as 'more' and 'fewer' to compare two quantities.

Resources: Plastic mirrors; eyes cut from white paper; crayons in eye colours; a noticeboard with axes and labels for the bar chart at child height (see diagram); Blu-tack.

Key vocabulary: Bar chart, colours for eye colours, numbers sufficient to count the eyes.

Organisation: Whole group.

What to do:

Whilst sitting in a circle on the floor talk about eye colours. Ask children in turn to say their eye colour. Where children are uncertain provide a mirror for them to check. Show the group the cut-out eyes. Explain that they will be used to make a record of their eye colours. Invite children in turn to select a crayon the same colour as their eyes and to go and colour their iris. Once coloured help children to stick their eye on the prepared bar chart. As a group use the bar chart to count how many children have each eye colour. Which colour do most children have? Do more children have blue or brown eyes?

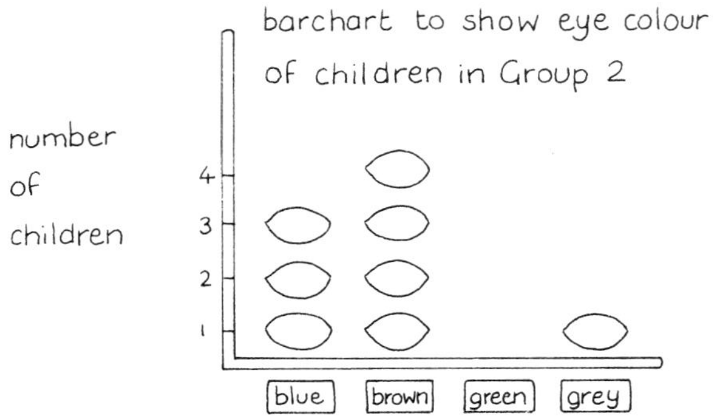

Activity: Optician role play area

Learning opportunity: Playing collaboratively in a role play situation.

Early Learning Goal: Creative Development. Children will use their imagination in play.

Resources: A role play area set out as an optician's with: a white coat/shirt; a telephone; a diary; a selection of toy spectacles; plastic sun spectacles and home made spectacles; a mirror; a letter chart; a till.

Key vocabulary: Spectacles, glasses, eye test.

Organisation: Whole group introduction with small groups using the area.

What to do:

Involve children in the setting up of the optician's. Let them make eye testing charts and spectacles. Introduce the area to the whole group and talk about the items in it. Talk about the way an optician tests eyesight and the importance of helping customers to buy spectacles that they will be happy to wear. Choose a small group to play in the optician's and over the coming days encourage all children to take on a variety of roles.

Display

Mount and display the children's paintings as an art gallery. Number the pictures and make a catalogue of titles suggested by the children.

Around the bar chart place question cards which encourage children to extract information. Ask how many children have each eye colour. Which colour do most children have? Near the role play area display the spectacles made by children with price labels and a mirror.

Week 5

Healthy week

Personal, Social and Emotional Development

- Talk about the importance of wearing the right types of clothes when playing outside during different times of the year. This can help to keep us healthy (see activity opposite). (PS10)
- Read *Oliver's Fruit Salad* by Vivian French (Hodder Children's Books) or/and *Oliver's Vegetables*. Talk about favourite foods. (PS1, 2, 4)
- Read *Sports Day* by Nick Butterworth and Mick Inkpen (Picture Knight). Talk about the importance of keeping fit. Encourage children to play active games during play times. (PS4)

Language and Literacy

- Set up the role play area as a healthy eating cafe. (L1)
- Read *The Shopping Basket* by John Burningham. (Red Fox). Which foods in the story would have been good to eat? Ask children to retell the story using the pictures as a reminder of events. (L3, 6)
- Make picture or word menus for the cafe. (L12, 13, 15)

Mathematics

- Provide each child with a cut-out of a shopping basket and a list of healthy foods for them to draw in their basket (for example, 4 apples, 2 carrots, 3 beakers of water). (M2, 3)
- Repeat the basket activity but this time draw in the foods and ask children to write on a shopping list how many there are of each. (M2, 3)
- Buy and sell food in the role play cafe. (M5, 11)

Knowledge and Understanding of the World

- Having first checked for children's food allergies, try taste testing for a variety of fruits and raw vegetables. (K1, 3)
- Talk about the kinds of foods which are good to eat. Provide each child with a sandwich box made from a piece of A4 card folded in half. Ask children to make healthy packed lunches either by cutting pictures out of magazines or by drawing. (K3)
- Talk about places in the local environment where children enjoy playing and ones which are disliked. Talk about safety, why the places are liked or disliked and how children might like to change them. (K10)

Physical Development

- Talk about the importance of gradually using different parts of our bodies in a warm-up before doing an activity which involves a lot of movement. Do a 'follow my leader' warm-up and talk about which parts of the body are being used (see activity opposite). (PD2, 4)
- Set up a variety of challenges which involve both fine motor and gross motor skills. Examples include spooning water from one container to another, threading beads, stacking cubes, catching a ball, dribbling a ball, jumping, skipping. Repeat these activities a number of times over the week and show children how practice can help us to improve. (PD6)
- Make healthy foods from playdough. (PD8)

Creative Development

- On paper plates use tissue paper to make a healthy meal. (C1)
- Weave place mats for the healthy cafe. (C1)
- Print with vegetables and hard fruits. (C1)

Activity: Warming up

Learning opportunity: Moving with control and following instructions.

Early Learning Goal: Physical Development. Children will move with control and co-ordination. They will recognise the importance of keeping healthy and things which contribute to this.

Resources: Large space.

Key vocabulary: Circle, fast, slow, quietly, parts of the body.

Organisation: Whole group.

What to do:

Sitting on the floor, talk to children about the importance of gradually warming up before they begin very active activities and games. Hold up a hand and ask children which parts can move. Do a variety of finger and wrist exercises and ask children to copy. Gradually continue with other parts of the body, encouraging children to recognise which parts are being exercised. Once all parts have been warmed up, play a favourite whole group game which involves running. Finally, cool down by playing sleeping lions where children lie on the ground as if asleep.

Activity: Wearing the right clothes

Learning opportunity: Picking and wearing clothes to suit a variety of weather conditions and temperatures.

Early Learning Goal: Personal, Social and Emotional Development. Children will dress and undress independently.

Resources: A large box containing a variety of items of clothing including ones for winter, wet and sunny weather such as a scarf, wellington boots, a sun hat and a raincoat; pictures of people dressed sensibly for a variety of weathers.

Key vocabulary: Names of clothing in the basket, wet, hot, cold, sunny, rainy, summer, winter.

Organisation: Whole group.

What to do:

Show the pictures of the people. Ask children what the people are wearing and why the items of clothing would be sensible ones to wear. Show the group the clothes that are in the basket. Ask a child to come and pick something which would be good to wear on a sunny day and to put it on. Ask why it would be good. What else would be useful on a sunny day? Repeat the activity for a variety of weathers and times of year. Encourage children to dress independently and to think of safety issues as well as the weather. For example, it would not be sensible to wear mittens if playing on a climbing frame. On a sunny day children should wear sun screen as well as sun hat.

Display

On a large board put up a paper tablecloth and make a picnic display with the paper plates of healthy foods. Display the playdough foods on a table in front.

On a second board, stick up the pictures showing people in a variety of clothing and place the basket of clothes nearby. Invite children to enjoy wearing them as they visit the healthy cafe and for their own choice of role play situations.

Week 6

Faces

Personal, Social and Emotional Development

- Talk about the 'Disguises day' which will take place at the end of the week and the jobs which will have to be done. (PS1, 2, 3)
- In circle time, talk about the importance of smiling. At the end of the session pass a smile around the circle (see activity opposite). (PS4, 6)
- Declare a 'Smile week' in which children will try to make people feel happy by smiling at them. (PS4, 6)

Language and Literacy

- Read *All Kinds of People* by Emma Damon (Ted Smart). (L3)
- Provide children with paper and magazines from which to cut out smiling faces to make 'Smile please!' posters. (L12, 15)
- Talk about the way our faces can show how we are feeling. Ask children to show you a sad face, a happy face, a sleeping face, an angry face and a frightened face. Make small books which have a face on the cover crying or smiling and inside have sentences beginning with either 'I am sad when ....' or 'I am happy when ....' (L9, 12, 13)

Mathematics

- Use the face as the stimulus for counting activities with a small group. Count how many ears, eyes, noses and mouths the group has. Encourage them to notice that the number of eyes is the same as the number of ears. As children begin to notice similarities, ask them to predict how many chins the group will have. (M2, 11)
- Provide children with drawings of half faces. Encourage them to complete the pictures to make symmetrical faces. Use plastic mirrors to check the faces are symmetrical. (M9, 10)
- Provide each child with a selection of sticky paper regular shapes. Ask them to make pictures of faces. Encourage the children to talk about the shapes they use for the eyes, nose, mouth and ears. (M10)

Knowledge and Understanding of the World

- Use mirrors to allow children to observe their own faces and then make paper-plate face masks. (K2, 3)
- Give descriptions of children to the group and ask them to say who you are describing. As you play, help children to realise the differences and similarities they have with peers. (K3)
- Make happy face mobiles by cutting card faces, decorating both sides and stringing them together (see diagram). (K5)

Physical Development

- Tell the story of a spy putting on his disguise and encourage children to mime to the story. (PD1)
- Play shadow games in which children are the spies who are trying to track you. Stress the importance of only moving when you move and trying to keep in your shadow. (PD 1, 2)
- Draw with chalk on the playground a variety of large faces with flowing hair. Use them for aiming games and for walking on the lines. (PD1, 2)

Creative Development

- Sing 'If you're happy and you know it clap your hands' in *Apusskido Songs for Children* (A & C Black). (C5)
- Make two-faced clown puppets which smile and cry from paper plates (see activity opposite). (C1, 4)
- Use pasta, string and wool to make collages of faces. These are particularly effective if they are sprayed with silver or gold paint when dry. (C1)

Activity: Smiling

Learning opportunity: Working collaboratively, listening to others and talking with feeling.

Early Learning Goal: Personal, Social and Emotional Development. Children will be aware of and sensitive to the feelings of others. They will show their feelings.

Resources: A hand puppet.

Key vocabulary: Smile, happy.

Organisation: Whole group sitting on the floor in a circle.

What to do:

Remind the group of the routine for circle time and the importance of always looking at the person who is speaking. Praise those who are already looking at you as you talk.

Show the group your puppet. Tell the group its name and that it is very special to you because whenever you see it you smile. Ask the children how they feel when someone smiles at them. What makes them smile?

Pass the puppet around the circle. Whoever holds the puppet has the opportunity to speak. Once all the children who want to have spoken, talk about the importance of smiles for helping us to feel good. Finish by 'passing a smile' around the circle.

Activity: Clown puppets

Learning opportunity: Using a variety of materials to make puppets and using the puppets in imaginative, role play situations.

Early Learning Goal: Creative Development. Children will explore colour and form and use their imagination in play.

Resources: Selection of scraps of material, paper, wool, sequins; felt pens; ready mixed paints; glue; scissors; an example of a paper-plate puppet clown. For each child: two small paper plates, two card triangles from which to make the hat and a thick 30cm long piece of dowelling or cardboard tubing.

Key vocabulary: Names of materials and colours being used, clown, happy, sad.

Organisation: Small group.

What to do:

Show the group the example of the clown puppet. Show them that it has two faces and ask why that would be useful in a play. Let the group ask the clown some questions.

Give each child a plate and ask them to draw a happy face on the underneath/non waxy side. Remind children of where they need to position the eyes. Repeat this with the sad face. Finally, stick strips of paper or wool on for hair. When dry, stick the plates together with glue with the dowelling/card tube stuck inside for the neck/handle.

Decorate the card triangles brightly and glue them on to the head. When completely dry, the children can use their puppets to make plays to perform for their friends.

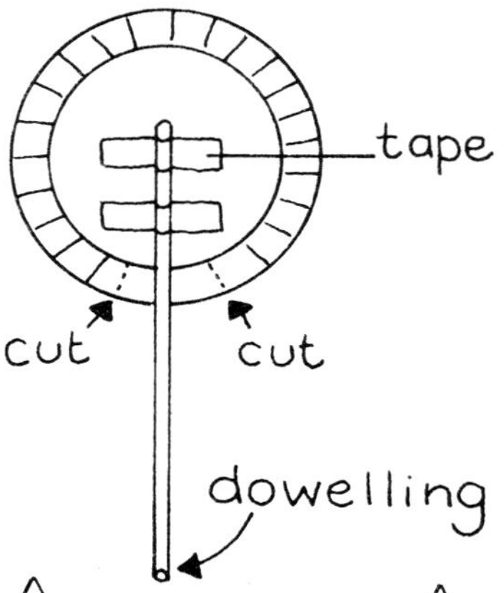

Display

Display the face collages with a 'Smile please!' poster on a board and hang the smiling mobiles close by. Cover a table with a drape and carefully place the clown puppets on it. To the side arrange a table or large box as a puppet theatre for children to use their puppets in. Also include a book of tickets and till so that children can sell tickets for their shows.

Bringing it all together

A day of disguises

Explain to the children that they are going to have 'A day of disguises'. They will learn how to disguise themselves. At the end there will be a special disguise parade to which parents and friends will be invited.

The event will work best if it is held in a large room/hall where a variety of activities can be set out for children to visit in turn. Divide the children into small groups of about four children with an adult. Give each child a piece of card which is set out as a passport to be completed during the event. Allocate each group to an activity and explain the direction in which they will move. Make sure that the adults have ideas for games such as 'I spy' which they could play with their group should an activity finish before it is time to move on. If enough adults are available it is useful to have each activity run by a different person whilst others move round with the children.

Activities

- Having first checked that children are not allergic to face paints, invite adults to come in and help give children a new look.
- Put out passport photograph sized pieces of paper and crayons for children to record their new face and stick it in the passport.
- Talk to children about the way people can often be recognised from a long way off by how they move. Challenge the children to try walking in a variety of ways as if they were someone else. Help them to practise the walk they will use in the disguise parade.
- Talk to children about their names and their ages. For their disguise they will need a new name and age. Help children to record these in their passports.
- Make a collection of clothes which children can dress up in for their disguise. Collect enough for children to be able to keep the clothes on for the whole event.
- Use an ink pad to record children's thumb and finger prints.
- Talk about clothes and the way we often recognise people from the things they wear. Make a collection of shoes owned by children in the group. Play a game in which children have to recognise their own shoes and then identify those of friends. Before playing, check that all shoes are named but cover the names up for the game.
- Give each child a sheet containing nine outlines of identical faces. Invite the children to add lines to disguise the faces.
- Invite a parent with a Polaroid camera to take instant photos of the complete disguise for the passports.

Food

Although food is not a requirement for a 'disguises event' most children and adults will enjoy some refreshments after the parade.

Involve the children in preparing food:

- Make face biscuits by using melted chocolate, icing tubes and sweets to decorate plain biscuits.
- Make a 'disguised cocktail' by mixing a selection of fruit juices and adding small pieces of cut-up soft fruits. Can children identify which fruits and juices are in the cocktail?

The parade

After all the disguise activities have been done, ask children to sit on the floor in a circle. Arrange chairs around the circle for parents and friends. Put on some quiet, background music to which children will enjoy parading, such as the theme music to the *Pink Panther.* Invite children in turn to tell everyone their new name and age, and to walk around the circle in role. Once all those who want to parade have done so, share the biscuits and fruit cocktail.

Resources

Resources to collect

- Pictures of faces from magazines.
- Sequins.
- Plastic mirrors.
- Kaleidoscopes.
- Periscopes.
- Clothes for making disguises.

Everyday resources

- Boxes, large and small for modelling.
- Papers and cards of different weights, colours and textures, such as sugar paper, corrugated card, silver and shiny papers.
- Dry powder paints for mixing and mixed paints for covering large areas such as card tree trunks.
- Different sized paint brushes from household brushes to thin brushes for delicate work and a variety of paint mixing containers.
- A variety of drawing and colouring pencils, crayons, pastels, charcoals, chalks.
- Additional decorative and finishing materials such as sequins, foil, glitter, tinsel, shiny wool and threads, beads, pieces of textiles, parcel ribbon.
- Table covers.
- Pasta.

Stories

Skeleton Crew by Allan Ahlberg and Andre Amstutz (Mammoth).

Funnybones by Janet and Allan Ahlberg (Picture Lions).

Look into their Eyes by Richard Brassey (Dolphin).

If At First You Do Not See by Ruth Brown (Beaver Books).

The Shopping Basket by John Burningham (Red Fox).

Sports Day by Nick Butterworth and Mick Inkpen (Picture Knight).

All Kinds of People by Emma Damon (Ted Smart).

Oliver's Fruit Salad by Vivian French (Hodder Children's Books).

Oliver's Vegetables by Vivian French (Hodder Children's Books).

Mr Little's New Car by Richard Fowler (Mammoth).

Peace at Last by Jill Murphy (Macmillan Children's Books).

Don't do that! by Tony Ross (Red Fox).

I Don't Want to go to Bed by Julie Sykes and Tim Warnes (Magi Publications).

Non-fiction

Feelings by Aliki (Piccolo Picture Books).

1001 Things to Spot on the Farm by Gillian Doherty (Usborne).

How I Breathe by Mandy Suhr (Wayland).

I am Growing by Mandy Suhr (Wayland).

I Can Move by Mandy Suhr (Wayland).

When I Eat by Mandy Suhr (Wayland).

Songs

Okki-tokki-unga Action Songs for Children chosen by Beatrice Harrop, Linda Friend and David Gadsby (A & C Black).

Apusskido Songs for Children chosen by Beatrice Harrop, Peggy Blakely and David Gadsby (A & C Black).

Poems

This Little Puffin by Elizabeth Matterson (Puffin).

Out and About by Shirley Hughes (Walker Books).

Collecting evidence of children's learning

Monitoring children's development is an important task. Keeping a record of children's achievements will help you to see progress and will draw attention to those who are having difficulties for some reason. If a child needs additional professional help, such as speech therapy, your records will provide valuable evidence.

Records should be the result of collaboration between group leaders, parents and carers. Parents should be made aware of your record keeping policies when their child joins your group. Show them the type of records you are keeping and make sure they understand that they have an opportunity to contribute. As a general rule, your records should form an open document. Any parent should have access to records relating to his or her child. Take regular opportunities to talk to parents about children's progress. If you have formal discussions regarding children about whom you have particular concerns, a dated record of the main points should be kept.

Keeping it manageable

Records should be helpful in informing group leaders, adult helpers and parents and always be for the benefit of the child. However, keeping records of every aspect of each child's development can become a difficult task. The sample shown will help to keep records manageable and useful. The golden rule is to keep them simple.

Observations will basically fall into three categories:

- **Spontaneous records:** Sometimes you will want to make a note of observations as they happen, for example, a child is heard counting cars accurately during a play activity, or is seen to play collaboratively for the first time.
- **Planned observations:** Sometimes you will plan to make observations of children's developing skills in their everyday activities. Using the learning opportunity identified for an activity will help you to make appropriate judgements about children's capabilities and to record them systematically.

To collect information:

- talk to children about their activities and listen to their responses;
- listen to children talking to each other;
- observe children's work such as early writing, paintings and 3D models. (Keeping photocopies or photographs is sometimes useful.)

Sometimes you may wish to set up 'one off' activities for the purposes of monitoring development. Some pre-school groups, for example, ask children to make a drawing of themselves at the beginning of each term to record their progressing skills in both co-ordination and observation. Do not attempt to make records after every activity!

- **Reflective observations:** It is useful to spend regular time reflecting on the progress of a few children (about four each week). Aim to make some brief comments about each child every half term.

Informing your planning

Collecting evidence about children's progress is time consuming and it is important that it is useful. When you are planning, use the information you have collected to help you decide what learning opportunities you need to provide next for children. For example, a child who has poor pencil control will benefit from more play with dough or construction toys to build the strength of hand muscles.

Example of recording chart

Name: Jonathan Hogg **D.O.B.** 18.2.94 **Date of entry:** 13.9.98

Term	Personal and Social	Language and Literacy	Mathematics	Knowledge and Understanding	Physical	Creative
ONE	Reluctant to say good bye to mother. Prefers adult company. 20.9.98 EMH	Enjoys listening to stories, particularly liked *Funnybones*. Can write first name. Good pencil control. 20.10.98 EMH	Is able to say numbers to ten and count accurately five objects. Recognises and names squares and circles. 5.11.98 BM	Keen to ask questions. Is fascinated by all facts about the body. 16.10.98 AC	Can balance on one leg. Loved trying to walk in different ways. Does not like the feel of playdough. 16.10.98 AC	Made a wonderful face collage. Enjoys painting, particularly mixing own colours. 20.10.98 LSS
TWO						
THREE						

Skills overview of six week plan

Week	Topic focus	Personal, Social and Emotional	Language and Literacy	Mathematics	Knowledge and Understanding of the World	Physical	Creative
1	Bits and pieces	Appreciating body parts	Listening Writing Book making	Comparative language Counting	Labelling body parts Constructing	Moving with control and imagination	Singing Painting Making sounds
2	Handy week	Listening to others; Taking turns; Developing independence	Describing Writing	Counting Comparing size Estimating	Making observations Comparing Describing	Catching Throwing Using malleable materials	Finger painting Singing
3	Listening week	Sensitivity to others Listening	Listening to stories Making a book Initial sounds; Rhyming	Comparative language; Shape Counting	Comparing similarities and differences	Moving with control and imagination	Dancing Playing instruments; Singing
4	Looking week	Taking turns	Using descriptive vocabulary; Letter formation; Talking	Language of shape Counting	Talking Investigating Observing	Aiming Moving with awareness of space	Using materials Painting Role play
5	Healthy week	Health awareness	Discussing Purposeful writing	Counting Using money	Using senses Environmental preferences	Moving with control; Using malleable materials	Weaving Collage
6	Faces	Expressing emotions Collaborative planning	Listening to a story Writing for a purpose Talking about feelings	Shape awareness Counting Symmetry	Observing Describing Using materials	Moving with imagination and control	Singing Collage Using tools

Home links

The theme of All About Me lends itself to useful links with children's homes and families. Through working together children and adults gain respect for each other and build comfortable and confident relationships.

Establishing partnerships

- Keep parents informed about the topic of All About Me and the themes for each week. By understanding the work of the group, parents will enjoy the involvement of contributing ideas, time and resources.
- Photocopy the parent's page for each child to take home.
- Invite friends, childminders and families to share all or part of the 'Day of disguises'.

Visiting enthusiasts

- Invite adults to come in to talk about wearing spectacles and contact lenses.
- Invite adults who enjoy face painting to run an activity at sthe disguises event.

Resource requests

- Ask parents to contribute clothes which are no longer needed for making disguises.
- Parcel bows, wrapping paper, wallpaper and any interesting boxes and packaging are invaluable for collage work and a wide range of interesting activities.

The day of disguises

- It is always useful to have extra adults at times such as the disguises event.
- Put out a suggestion box in which parents can contribute ideas for activities which could be used on the day of disguises.
- Invite parents to donate games such as 'Misfits' which fit with the disguises theme.